SEMINAR STUDIES IN HISTORY

Editor: Patrick Richardson

THE ESTABLISHED CHURCH AND POPULAR RELIGION 1750–1850

SEMINAR STUDIES IN HISTORY

Editor: Patrick Richardson

A full list of titles in this
series will be found on the
back cover of this book

SEMINAR STUDIES IN HISTORY

THE ESTABLISHED CHURCH AND POPULAR RELIGION 1750–1850

Alan Smith

Senior History Master
The Coopers' Company's School

1971

LONGMAN

LONGMAN GROUP LIMITED
London

ASSOCIATED COMPANIES, BRANCHES AND
REPRESENTATIVES THROUGHOUT THE WORLD

© Longman Group Ltd 1971

First published 1970
ISBN 0 582 31464 X

PRINTED IN GREAT BRITAIN BY
WESTERN PRINTING SERVICES LTD, BRISTOL

Contents

INTRODUCTION TO THE SERIES   vii

Part One · The Background

1 THE PERIOD UNDER REVIEW   3
2 ANGLICANISM   8
3 THE DISSENTERS   15
4 SUPERSTITIONS AND PREJUDICES   19

Part Two · The Church and its Rivals

5 THE CHURCH AWARE   25
6 THE IMPACT OF METHODISM   33
7 SECTARIAN MOVEMENTS   41
8 EVANGELICALS AND JACOBINS   51
9 THE HIGH CHURCH REVIVAL   57

Part Three · Assessment and Aftermath   71

Part Four · Documents   77

BIBLIOGRAPHY   111

INDEX   118

Introduction to the Series

The seminar method of teaching is being used increasingly. It is a way of learning in smaller groups through discussion, designed both to get away from and to supplement the basic lecture techniques. To be successful, the member of a seminar must be informed, or else—in the unkind phrase of a cynic—it can be a 'pooling of ignorance'. The chapter in the textbook of English or European history by its nature cannot provide material in this depth, but at the same time the full academic work may be too long and perhaps too advanced.

For this reason we have invited practising teachers to contribute short studies on specialised aspects of British and European history with these special needs in mind. For this series the authors have been asked to provide, in addition to their basic analysis, a full selection of documentary material of all kinds and an up-to-date and comprehensive bibliography. Both these sections are referred to in the text, but it is hoped that they will prove to be valuable teaching and learning aids in themselves.

Note on the System of References:

A bold number in round brackets (**5**) in the text refers the reader to the corresponding entry in the Bibliography section at the end of the book.

A bold number in square brackets, preceded by 'doc.' [**docs 6, 8**] refers the reader to the corresponding items in the section of documents, which follows the main text.

PATRICK RICHARDSON
General Editor

Part One

THE BACKGROUND

1 The Period under Review

The period 1750 to 1850 is a distinctive one in the history of the Established Church. It is the age when the Church accepted *total* identification with the existing social fabric; an age of the most complete Erastianism and of entire subservience to the purposes of government. The prorogation of Convocation from 1741 to 1855 perhaps symbolically defines the limits of the period more exactly—though one may plausibly argue that not until after the '45 had the Hanoverian Church–State complex proved its absolute viability.

The origin of this ecclesiastical situation must be sought in the political events of 1688, for then it was that the Tories were forced by the conduct of James II to make a choice between their Anglican Church and their Stuart King. By far the greater part of them preferred their Church and so acquiesced in the new regime of William and Mary. The reign of Anne was for them a happy reunion of Stuart monarchy with an active, self-confident Church of England, so self-confident in fact that its Dissenting allies of 1688 could be barred from their well established practice of Occasional Conformity (1711) and threatened with extinction as a community by the banning of their schools (Schism Act 1714). The Society for the Promotion of Christian Knowledge (1698) the Society for the Propagation of the Gospel, (1701) the 1710 Commission for building new churches in London (to which we owe Hawksmoor's six English Baroque masterpieces), the Charity School movement, parochial libraries, the Society for the Reformation of Manners—all these speak of a vigorous outreaching Church—but in 1714 the conservative churchman had again to make an invidious choice; to restore the male Stuarts on grounds of legitimacy and risk the overthrow of Anglicanism or preserve his Church under Hanoverian auspices and (if a Tory) suffer indefinite exclusion from power, for

George's appointment of his Lords Justices and later of his first ministry showed his plain identification of his own interests with those of the Whigs alone. Thus it was that the Hanoverian Church–State relationship came into being. To oppose the new monarchy was held to imply preference for an antinational policy of Roman Catholic obscurantism. The Church leadership saw its only safety in backing the Whigs. The Whigs used the Church as an instrument of social and political control. The logic of this situation was to identify churchmanship with good citizenship. The dangerous instabilities of any 'enthusiasm' (in its eighteenth-century sense of fanaticism) were deplored. For a time at least the Church accepted its minor role in a politically conceived greater scheme of things.

It has been noted as 'a strange paradox' that 'though the workaday religion preached and practised by the mass of the clergy . . . has rarely been so uninspiring as in this century, yet few ages in our history have been so prolific in serious thought about the fundamentals and justification of the whole scheme of Christianity and especially of the Established Church itself' (**5**). This was a great age of religious controversy. Long used to defending himself against the apologists of Rome or of traditional dissent the Anglican now had to face the challenge of Deism, which argued against the plausibility or even the necessity of any revealed religion. Another critical tendency culminated in the pure scepticism of Hume. In parallel to these, though largely as an autonomous trend exemplified by men like Samuel Clarke and Whiston, ran streams of Arianism, Socinianism and Unitarianism. Dissenters and non-jurors naturally assailed the idea of Establishment, but the most violent controversy on this theme developed within the Church itself. In 1717 Bishop Hoadley of Bangor had preached on the text 'My kingdom is not of this world', and had argued that no existing earthly institution could justifiably exercise valid religious authority. Uproar followed, some two hundred pamphlets resulted, and it required the suppression of Convocation to still the partisan strife of an angry Church. By 1750, however, this particular storm had abated.

The Anglicanism that could produce the subtle philosophy of Berkeley, the piety of Law and the judicious highmindedness of Butler was quite capable of conducting its own spiritual and intellectual defence without the aid of any secular arm, yet in the sphere of practical administration this same Church was woefully blind and its own worst enemy. The Methodist revival associated with John Wesley can very properly be considered as a return to the methods of the 1670s when religious societies were in vogue. There is no doubt as to John Wesley's loyalty to the established order of things whether political or ecclesiastical, nor is there any doubt as to his profoundly felt orthodoxy. His triumphant movement might well have been deemed the inflowing of the Spirit for which the Anglican vessel had been prepared. The Church, however, as a church, did nothing to encourage and much to discourage this free-will offering of devoted lives. The contrast between Rome's treatment of the Franciscans and Canterbury's of the Methodists has often been commented on (**31**) for the comparison between the two movements is a close one (**29**). All that needs to be noted here is that this promising movement, which struck genuine roots among the common people, was allowed to drift out of the orbit of the Establishment and compelled by shortsighted opponents to register its meeting places as dissenting chapels and its ministers as dissenting preachers. [**doc. 13b**]. As they were named, though not by their own choice, so in the next generation they largely considered themselves to be [**doc. 8b**]. In this way, the State Church's own Act of Toleration was used to create a quite unnecessary schism (**18**). The nature of Methodism and of its impact on society has been the subject of much discussion (**17, 32, 36**) but there is general agreement that if at first it was 'a religion for the poor, not of the poor' it did become a genuine church of the people. The 'Primitive' revival of the early nineteenth century—that repetition, or should we say parody?—of the Methodist phenomenon was, it has never been doubted, both for the people and of them from the very first.

The political earth tremors initiated by the French Revolution were not without their effects on religious life. Within the Established Church the Evangelicals sought both to purify the spiritual life of the nation (by personal example as well as by Act of Parliament) and to conduct an impassioned defence of the existing social order. Halevy (**4**) writes, 'Never in the history of Anglicanism had any party exercised so profound an influence. Never had any party been in such a false position.' Whatever the Evangelicals did for the outward life of the masses through their proximity to the seats of power, they struck no popular roots and if anything only nurtured the anticlericalism they abhorred as a fruit of Jacobinism and atheism [**docs. 17, 20, 21**]. Popular religious sentiment at this time found greater interest in the apocalyptic fantasies of Richard

Brothers 'God Almighty's Nephew', or in the teachings of the prophetess Joanna Southcott, who though she bore no Messiah was a prolific mother of sectarianism. Even the obscure sect of the Muggletonians underwent modest revivals in time of national crisis (e.g. 1756, 1832, 1846). The end of the French wars brought a revival of liberal sentiment, inaugurated by the reconstruction of the Tory ministry in 1822, which swept away the remnants of discrimination against the Dissenters (Repeal of Test and Corporation Acts 1828) and admitted Roman Catholics to Parliament (1829). It reached its peak with the Grey ministry of 1830 which, having reformed the national legislature, sparked off new controversy when it logically undertook an administrative overhaul of the national Church (52). In 1833 a modest plan to divert some of the surplus revenues of the Irish bishops provoked John Keble to preach his famous 'National Apostasy' sermon indicting Parliament of 'direct disavowal of the sovereignty of God'. Such verbal extravagance might in other ages have gone unnoticed. In its actual context it led to a serious reconsideration of the true nature of authority in religion. Both Brethrenism and the Catholic Apostolic Church (the so called Irvingites) arose as byproducts of this debate, but its major result was the Tractarian or Oxford Movement, a rather selfconscious and very academic reaction away from the world of rationalist Whiggery towards the Middle Ages. Tractarianism at first had little direct effect on the faith and practice of the broad masses, though it did convulse the internal politics of the Church. The revival of Convocation in the 1850s symbolises the newer 'Oxford' concept of the Church as an independent estate of the realm.

The Church of England in the 1840s still retained much of the strength it had possessed in the Hanoverian age. It still carried with it, for most people, an air of ineluctable legitimacy. Even among 'hard line' Dissenters marriage and burial by the rites of the Established Church was common. It was the focus of much popular superstition and fringe magic [**doc. 10**]. It exercised a strong gravitational pull on all who sought social acceptance by the manifestly established and successful. (It was proverbial that a Dissenter's second horse would take him to the parish church.) The Established Church controlled most of what educational system there was and its grip on the older universities was as yet unchallenged. It comprised a broad spectrum of theological beliefs, practised a wide tolerance and was even, at the fringes, accommodating itself to 'socialism'. It could still produce saints and scholars enough to vindicate its own cause yet it can only be conceded that the combined forces of Church and State had made as little real mark on many of the urban English as it had on the rural [**docs. 19, 29, 30**]. The Ecclesiastical Titles Bill of 1851, passed in response to so called 'Papal agression' seems a half-hearted attempt to start old hares. Far more significant was that year's unique Census of Religious Worship (**55**) which records objectively enough the measurable results of a hundred years of identification of Church and State. The issues of the next century were to be quite different in kind: Genesis *v.* Darwin, the recognition of working-class alienation, the development of a social gospel, the fight against sheer indifference. The old simplistic identification of 'Church and King', or of 'liberties, property and [Anglican] religion' was gone, utterly gone.

2 Anglicanism

WHAT IT MEANT TO BE AN ANGLICAN

'Glory be to Thee, O Lord my God, who hast made me a member of this Church of England whose faith and government and worship are holy and Catholic and Apostolic and free from all extremes of irreverence and superstition and which I firmly believe to be a sound part of the Church Universal and which teaches me charity to those who dissent from me' (A prayer of Bishop Thomas Ken, d.1711).

This quiet confidence, not without its suggestion of complacency, is characteristic of Anglicanism in the period under our review. [**docs. 1, 4**]. The Church of England, once embattled against Pope and Puritan, had survived the crisis of '45 and could now relax and enjoy its security. It was the Church of a well established ruling class, the Church of a vast majority of citizens. Its sacrament was the official test of loyalty to the political regime—and indeed to the very social order. (Readers of Smollett may recall the horror expressed by the ship's chaplain when he heard that Roderick Random—a humble surgeon's mate—was a Presbyterian; 'At this word the chaplain expressed great astonishment, and said he could not apprehend how a Presbyterian was entitled to any post under the English government. Then he asked if I had ever received the sacrament or taken the oaths; to which questions I replying in the negative, he held up his hands and assured me he could do me no service, wished I might not be in a state of reprobation, and returned to his messmates'). Only Anglicans, or those who could plausibly pass as such could (without penalty) aspire to office in national or local government, hold commissions in the armed forces or graduate at the universities. Apart from those of the Jews and the Quakers (two inconsiderable though obstinate minorities) only marriages celebrated by Anglican rites were legally valid. The same great families who administered the state ruled the Church.

We find a Cornwallis as archbishop, Keppels, Barringtons and a Norris as bishops. In 1815 eleven of the English Episcopal Bench (there were two archbishops and twenty-six bishops) were of noble birth. Those who were not were invariably friends, dependents (or creatures) of those who wielded political power. The Church of Ireland, with its extravagant establishment of four archbishops and twenty-seven bishops, was in the same condition. The notorious Bishop of Clogher was the son of an earl. One great family alone, the Beresfords, held three Irish sees. In these circumstances there was no possibility of rivalry between Church and State. They were obverse and reverse of the same coin. The only likely rift was between bishops appointed by different regimes. When Stanhope launched his attack on the Occasional Conformity and Schism Acts he was opposed by fifteen bishops who were High Tory creations in the reign of Anne. Those in favour were a composite group— two appointed by William III, three by Anne and six by George I. As the Hanoverian regime established itself, the episcopal bench assumed a more homogeneous—or servile!—character.

The political nature of episcopal appointment was not the only bond between the Church and *le pays légal*. The dominant landlord class had the right of presentation (nominating the vicar) in half the parishes of England and Wales. The Church itself—though not as a Church, for corporate life was at a low ebb—but through individual bishops or cathedral chapters—presented the clergy to perhaps one parish in ten. The rest were accounted for by corporate bodies— colleges of the Universities or public schools—or by the Crown. There was yet a third correspondence between the ecclesiastical and social structures. If many of the higher clergy were nobles, all had to be gentlemen, for all had to have graduated at the university. It is true that their classical knowledge might be slight and that the bishop's requirement for their ordination might be minimal (James Woodforde was untypical in being examined by the Bishop of Oxford's chaplain for as long as half an hour) (**13**), but they shared the educational background of the other professions. The clerical calling was simply one possible choice for the young man of good family. Jane Austen's young men often balanced the possibilities of the Church against those of the army. Gibbon put the law, trade, public office, the East India Company and 'the fat slumbers of the Church' much on a par with each other. The Church was more often a career than a vocation.

9

The prizes of the Church—and they were not inconsiderable—were awarded on the same principle as those of the State—for political loyalty, distinguished services, or for having interest with the mighty. If the great men of the Church were also those of the State, the humble curates too were at one with their social circle. Fielding's Mr Trulliber was 'a parson on Sundays but all the other six might more properly be called a farmer' (*Joseph Andrews*, chap. 14). In 1806, Wilberforce cited the case of a curate-weaver (**4**), while at Lastingham (Yorks) the Rev. Mr Carter, with thirteen children and a stipend of £20 per annum, supplemented his living by angling. His wife kept a public house and the curate was able to convince his archdeacon that this indirect clerical management (and, it seems some direct clerical fiddle playing) caused the parishioners to be 'imperceptibly led along the path of piety and morality' (**61**). Within what sort of an organisation did these clergy, whether great or small function? It was, like much else in England a crazy jumble of ancient and *ad hoc* (**4, 7, 8, 30**). Its diocesan structure was geographically uneven and arbitrary. The diocese of Bristol, for example, was in two detached portions and that of Bangor in three. Lincoln had some 1,300 parishes, Carlisle only 100. Episcopal incomes varied wildly. In 1815 Durham was worth £19,000 a year while Llandaff was worth £900. The poorer bishops augmented their incomes by holding other ecclesiastical offices—deaneries or ordinary benefices—in plurality. It was, despite the obvious bad consequences, a recognised method of levelling up the grosser inequalities. At parish level the same method was also used with even worse consequences. A man of influence drew the income, a starving curate did the work for a pittance. One third of all the livings of England and Wales were worth less than £50 a year [**doc. 4**]. Small wonder that Mr Carter of Lastingham needed his fiddle and his fishing rod, or that Trulliber fed his hogs.

What was taught and what was believed by this oddly managed Church? Its formal creed was embodied in the Thirty-nine Articles but provided this belief was formally affirmed at ordination or induction to a benefice, no detailed interpretation was insisted on. Gisborne, an author of our period argued thus: 'The point . . . which the candidate for Orders has to decide is the nature of the subscription which will satisfy the intention of the Legislature existing at the time.' Questions of theology were hardly thought to be involved. It was conformity for conformity's sake; a general assent to a system. Halévy (4) bluntly puts it: 'The material point was that no one was really obliged to believe the Thirty-nine Articles, or even to read them.' The Feathers Tavern petitioners of 1772 who worried about those who might have scruples in these matters were simply men of too delicate a conscience for the age in which they lived.

Certainly the Church displayed no inquisitorial tendencies at this time. The prevailing spirit was that of Latitudinarianism, the prevailing tone that of reason. 'Reason is our universal law,' wrote William Law the mystic, 'that obliges us in all places and at all times; and no actions have any honour, but so far as they are instances of our obedience to reason' (*Serious Call* xxiv). Johnson said: 'We may take Fancy for a companion, but must follow Reason as our guide.' It was the general attitude of the time but we must suspect that the high philosophical reason of Law and Johnson was not always the reason of the ordinary incumbent who too often aimed at far too low a target. James Woodforde in August 1762, for example, noted a sermon 'concerning Private Interest giving way to Publick Good in regard to our having a Water Engine to prevent fire spreading' (13). This was the voice of reason at the grass roots, not only regularly unambitious, but too often merely tedious as well.

> By our pastor perplext
> How shall we determine?
> Watch and pray, says the text.
> Go to sleep, says the sermon. (8, p. 333)

In theory, services took place twice each Sunday with a sermon at morning and evening service alternately but in 1745 less than half the churches of the diocese of York had their two services [e.g. **doc. 4**] and in 1799 Arthur Young was noting the celebration of Divine Service only once a month (**87**, p. 438). Col. John Byng at Cheltenham in 1781 complained of the laziness of the Established Church but still believed 'thither would the people flock were pluralities in general abolished and more spiritual comfort to be had'. The vicar he noted had a stipend of £40 a year which he augmented by his skill at whist (**8**, p. 35). Eight years later he is still writing in the same strain (p. 218) '. . . the greater clergy do not attend regularly, or to any effect, or comfort.' Sometimes the mechanism seems to have broken down entirely, as at Tattersall in 1791. Contemplating the plundered Collegiate Church Byng wrote:

One might suppose (without any indelicate reflexion upon our bishops and their well ordered dioceses) that visitations were never made or questions about churches never asked. Else might not a bishop ask—'To whom belongeth this chancell? Who removed the windows; and the flooring, and the monuments of the dead? Why standeth not the altar at the proper place? Let everything be replaced and repaired with decency; so as to keep out the shame, and cold.' (**8**, p. 349)

To be an Anglican then meant to be involved in an intermittently functioning machine, yet despite the many difficulties that beset it (the political involvement, the crazy administrative system, the complacency) the machine did function, and often to some purpose. Triennial visitations were held and enormous numbers often presented themselves for confirmation. Archbishop Drummond of York confirmed over 40,000 in one visitation, as did Bishop Keppel of Exeter. The sacrament was celebrated monthly in towns, sometimes weekly in London, but in the country three to four times a year was the norm. The abuses identified as fit objects for attention by the Evangelical reformers in many ways give us a living picture of the Anglican Church in its Erastian heyday: too few churches (and had they all been filled only a fraction of the population could have been accommodated) non-resident vicars, underpaid curates and parsonage houses occupied by such socially acceptable if thoroughly unevangelical characters as (at worst) 'Parson Dolittle and Parson Merryman', or at best Cognatus [**doc. 3**]. We cannot expect the Evangelicals to have criticised that view of the Church that saw it as an essential defence of the social order against barbarism, yet implicit in this view is the complacency that was a vice of the age. Johnson is said to have declined a benefice in Lincolnshire because he held the essential duty of a clergyman to be 'the assiduous and familiar instruction of the vulgar and ignorant', while Addison had made the same point at the beginning of the century: 'It is certain that the Country-People would soon degenerate into a kind of Savages and Barbarians, were there not such frequent returns of a stated Time, in which the whole village meet together . . . to converse with one another on indifferent subjects . . . hear their Duties explained, and join together in Adoration of the supreme Being.' (**60**) It is a fair epitome of the religious aims of the Erastian Century [**doc. 5**].

To be an Anglican in this age was to be involved in an institution the shortcomings of which were patent and blatant. John Wesley knew them well and winced at 'the formal drawling of the parish clerk, the screaming of boys who bawl out what they neither feel nor understand' (**88**, iii p. 227). Yet this same Wesley, at the end of his long life could affirm as strongly as he was able his love for and loyalty to the Church of England.

This rickety and one would think scarcely seaworthy ark was for vast numbers of people the vessel of salvation, and the sentiments of Bishop Ken's prayer ('holy and Catholic and Apostolic and free from all extremes of irreverence and superstition and which I firmly believe to be a sound part of the Church Universal . . .') were those of many conscientious and (even if unambitiously so) truly good people.

THE NONJURORS

The nonjurors were a curious anomaly in the socioreligious struc-ture of the period. In 1688 a number of High Church bishops—five of the famous seven tried at the command of James II and including Sancroft the Archbishop of Canterbury—refused on grounds of conscience to take the oath of allegiance to the new regime and for this political offence were deprived of their offices. Some parish clergy and their congregations supported them in their stand. Ken, perhaps the best known of the group, found a patron and a refuge at Longleat, while Sancroft retired to his own estate at Fressingfield in Suffolk and there organised a new hierarchy for his holy remnant. There seems to be a (fortuitous?) association between the nonjurors and East Anglia; Sancroft at Fressingfield, Lloyd ex-Bishop of Norwich and Hickes 'bishop of Thetford'. At most the adherents of this *petite Eglise* numbered 20,000, but their secession was a real blow, however transient its effects, to the morale of the Establishment. Internal controversies over questions of ritual and discipline weakened the movement, but for most Anglicans the point of conscience on which it depended was so fine as to be almost imperceptible. Bishop Ken, for example, would not take the oath himself yet did not urge others to refuse it. Sancroft had seen the practical necessity for opposition to James and was willing enough to accept William as Regent though not as *de jure* king. For practical

purposes the law saw nonjurors as something akin to 'papists'—
they were, for example, subjected to the same penal tax of five
shillings in the pound at the time of Layer's conspiracy in 1722—
and this identification was not without some justification for, taking
the list of twenty-four Jacobite executions in the Newgate Calender
as our sample, nonjurors make the second largest group, providing
five identifiable victims to the Roman Catholics' twelve. Yet for all
this they were, at the top at least, seeking to maintain a genuine
spiritual integrity. Between 1716 and 1725 nonjurors were exploring
the possibility of communion with the Eastern Church and their
enquiries elicited one of the major statements of the Orthodox Faith
(**86**). However, nothing came of this contact. After the '45 the sect
began to languish, *pari passu* with Jacobitism itself, and by the
accession of George III it was virtually dead. The last 'bishop' of
the nonjurors died in 1805, not long before Cardinal York, last of
the direct Jacobite line.

3 The Dissenters

'I was a Dissenter, and by some in Tolpuddle it is considered as the sin of witchcraft; nay, there is no forgiveness for it in this life nor that which is to come' (George Loveless, *The Victim of Whiggery* 1837). 'When I mean religion, I mean the Christian religion; and not only the Christian religion, but the Protestant religion; and not only the Protestant religion, but the Church of England,' (Mr Thwackum in Henry Fielding's *Tom Jones*, 1749). 'Dissent . . . a foolish habit that clung greatly to families in the grocery and chandlering lines, though not incompatible with prosperous wholesale dealing' (George Eliot, *The Mill on the Floss*, 1860).

These quotations strikingly portray the faces of Anglicanism most often seen by the Dissenter. In times of social crisis the Dissenter was the archetype of subversion. In times of stability he was simply 'not one of us', not so much tolerated by any active principle as merely allowed to exist out of what one authority (**15**) has called a spirit of 'patronising laziness'. The same writer also adopts a biblical metaphor to express rather a more charitable view of Anglican–Dissenter relationships: 'The lions of the Establishment suffered the lambs of dissent to lie down quietly with them—at a proper distance'. But this is in some way a grotesque reversal of appropriate symbolism for was it not Cromwell (Sir Ernest Barker's 'epitome of Nonconformity') who had been enthusiastically hailed as 'old lion' in a tribute of 1653 (**73**, p. 320)? The Dissenters were, not without some justification, long feared as a dangerous body of crypto Republicans and fanatics [**doc. 7**]. In this mood most Anglicans agreed with the simple proposition of James I, 'No bishop, no king' and with Roger L'Estrange who had written, 'Toleration of religion is cousin germane to a licence for rebellion.' (**18**, p. 116)

Attitudes to dissent obviously varied greatly from time to time and from place to place, but so far as the early years of the eighteenth century are concerned the image of the humble and mealy-mouthed moralist hawking his conscience among his reprobate fellow citizens has very little relevance. The generation of Bunyan's Greatheart and Valiant for Truth might have passed away but surely cannot have been forgotten by their sons and grandsons. Dissenters were feared. Their church was the church of a minority (**4, 5**) but it had been a church militant in the literal sense of the words. Nine out of ten Englishmen might be conforming Anglicans but, as Cromwell had once pertinently asked, 'What if the tenth man be armed?' Suspicion of the Dissenters never wholly disappeared in the period under our review. It merely abated or was qualified or again rekindled with the changing balance of religious, social and political forces. The militant Puritans had appealed to the judgment of events. At the Restoration the lots had plainly fallen unfavourably. The Act of Uniformity saw the ejectment of some 2,000 clergy from the Church of England, perhaps one-fifth of the ministerial body, and the same Cavalier Parliament that inflicted this wound on the Church drew up a code of penal legislation that moulded the hard core Dissenters into 'an unshakeable feature of the social scene' though one set upon the far side of 'a gulf between Church and chapel which had lasted down to our own day' (**18**).

By 1689 when the Toleration Act was devised it had become obvious that laws incapable of distinguishing Catholic from Protestant nonconformists were in need of some revision. The Toleration Act exempted most Protestant Dissenters from certain legal penalties provided they gave what the law deemed to be adequate assurances of their purely political loyalty. Of course Nonconformists accepted the Revolution in preference to the rule of James II, just as they would accept the Hanoverians as against the Pretender. No other choice was conceivable. The Toleration Act was a justified experiment in treating the dissenters as men of 'scrupulous conscience' rather than as a group of political dissidents. It endeavoured to offer 'an effective means to unite their Majesties' protestant subjects in interest and affection'. It substantially succeeded. Yet, so strong was the Established Church, so deep-rooted the fear of the 'outsider' that the basic structure of the penal laws lasted into the nineteenth century, though the effort to extend them beyond their original scope by the Occasional Conformity and Schism Acts was only shortlived. Dissenters who risked life and property in defence of the dynasty during the '15 or the '45 received only, as Fox pointed out, 'an act of indemnity—a pardon for doing their duty as good citizens in rescuing their country in the hour of danger and distress'(**5**).

The anomaly was a gross one and the Anglican response to it was paradoxical. The official point of view was well defined by George III in 1772 when an alteration in the status of Dissenters was under discussion. He said: 'There is no shadow for this petition, as the Crown regularly grants a Nolle prosequi if any over-nice Justice of the Peace encourages prosecutions.' The sword of discrimination must remain as a symbol of legitimate Anglican dominance, but equally, by a gentleman's agreement, would remain sheathed!

Not all public authorities were as fairminded as the Crown in this respect. Until stopped by a decision of Lord Mansfield in 1767 the Corporation of London had mercilessly exploited wealthy Dissenters by nominating them for City offices knowing they could not conscientiously comply with the Anglican 'test' and then fining them for refusing to serve. The practice, however, continued at local level. As late as 1819 the officials of Mile End Old Town (East London) were seeking to compel Thomas Urquhart, a well-known Dissenter, to serve as churchwarden or be fined. At first his counter offer to find a substitute and pay £10 to a charity was refused though a Town's Meeting later accepted (**85**, pp. 13, 41, 42).

As the eighteenth century progressed the fires of Dissent burned low. As a political force they had shot their bolt; as a social force they had largely, except among the Quakers and Unitarians, lost their fervour. As individuals who turned to their own advantage their exclusion from the universities and the public service, they took a lead in education, technology and industry out of all proportion to their numbers. Dissenters flourished though Dissent languished. See (**7**) on the 'wretched economic situation of Dissenting ministers'. Steven Watson (**15**, p. 12) summarises thus: 'They were in the grip of a social order so strong they had ceased for a while to dream of smashing it.' The rising tide of rationalism, which merely caused the Anglican to trim his intellectual sails, took from many a Dissenter his very *raison d'être*. There seemed to be no choices other than decomposition and petrifaction (**4**). Slowly a drift to the Establishment began. Dissent gave a Harley to the State and a Ryder to the law, a Butler and a Secker to the Church. As we shall see later George Loveless perhaps spoke more bitterly than a deeper view of the Anglican–Dissenter dialogue would justify, for the separated parts of the Broad Church that existed before 1662 still held some communion with each other, but the most typical attitude of the Anglican Church to those Protestants outside its fellowship is well expressed by that definition allegedly offered by Bishop Warburton to Lord Sandwich; 'Orthodoxy, my lord, is my doxy; heterodoxy is another man's doxy.' This is the smug voice of the 'in grouper' who naturally thinks in terms of 'us' and 'them'. Dissenters were often not considered as a *religious* group at all [**doc. 6** and also the George Eliot quotation above]. Among those who did so consider them, however, attitude was usually a reflection of 'party'. The evangelically orientated London Society for the Conversion of the Jews might record its gratitude to 'dissenting gentleman' . . . 'actuated by principles of the most exalted philanthropy and liberality' (Appendix to 7th Report, 1815), but to Newman the word had very different associations. 'Had I been born in Dissent,' he wrote, 'perhaps I should never have been baptised; had I been born an English Presbyterian, perhaps I should never have known our Lord's divinity' (**56**, p. 268). Or again on an earlier occasion, 'There is not a Dissenter living but, inasmuch and so far as he dissents, is in a sin' (**9**, p. 236). One begins to feel the force of those words of Loveless with which we began [**doc. 8**].

4 Superstitions and Prejudices

'All as ever I larnt were the Creed, the Commandments and the Lord's Prayer, an' I war thout fit to go thru the world, tho' I didna know what any on 'em meant, ony the letter loike': an old man at the first farm labourers' conference in 1872 at Leamington (**82**, p. 27).

The Church of England was too little of an 'alma mater' to too many of her children, this much is clear. Her attitude to not only the secular but also the spiritual education of the masses was perfunctory and unsystematic. The old farm labourer's words are a very fair summary of one side of this relationship yet, somehow, the Church, at least in the eyes of the rural masses, never lost its spiritual magic. I use the word magic with intention. It is the only possible word in this context. Unsatisfactory though the Church may have been as a social agency or a teaching institution, slave of the state though it was, it was yet a psychic power house and often indeed a veritable pharmacopoeia. Baptism, for example, was often considered to be of physical as well as of spiritual benefit (**20**, p. 183 for sources and modern examples). Such was the fear of ritual uncleanness that to undergo the 'churching' ceremony—for all its official name of 'the Thanksgiving of Women after Childbirth'—was a social necessity for a new mother wishing to resume her place, however humble, in the community. Confirmation, though only if the recipient were lucky enough to be touched by the bishop's right hand, was a folk remedy for rheumatism. Pieces chipped from the statues of Exeter Cathedral were ground to powder and used with grease as a treatment for breast cancer. Lead scraped from the church windows during a service or cut from the water spouts at midnight had its 'medical' uses, as had scrapings of church bells, moss from the churchyard cross or even rainwater from the church roof. The vicar himself was often deemed to have a healing touch and a mixture of all the household's medicine dregs was known as 'Dean and Chapter' and thought to be a sovereign remedy (**19, 20**). It is perhaps in connection with these quite uncanonical supernatural powers that we may explain the odd usage of, for example, the Kendal area where clergy were subject to what educated people thought was an arbitrary distinction in title. The country people spoke of *Parson* Airey of Hugil but always of *Priest* Strickland of Staveley (**21**). This same source quotes a certain Canon Humble as follows: 'It is quite generally admitted that a priest may go anywhere and at any time of day or night and he will never be molested it if be known what he is.' But was it his cloth or his 'mana' that protected him?

The parish church was undoubtedly the focus of the community's faith—but what was the faith of the community? Very often a simple paganism seems to have lived on with the most nominal Christian colouring. Were the Cornishmen who practised strange rites at the Men-an-tol (a holed standing stone near Penzance) really more pagan than those who came at midnight to go three times round or three times under the church communion table (**69**, p. 160, **77**, p. 145)? Even without going into such questions as that of the use of the sacrament for purposes of witchcraft or of the steady demand for the clergy to carry out exorcisms it is obvious that the real beliefs of the countryman at this time embraced much more than our labourer's creed, commandments and Lord's Prayer.

The practices mentioned above were, for the most part, discouraged, even if not positively opposed by the clergy, but there were others which incumbents noted simply as curious local traditions (**21** *passim*). It is recorded in places as far apart as Essex, Hereford and Warwickshire that it was normal in our period for men to sit on one side of the church and women on the other, and a strange couple attempting to sit together in Abingdon Church were told by the verger, 'We don't have no sweethearting here!' The custom of bowing to the altar and of taking the communion fasting were deeply rooted folkways that had hardly died out before they were revived again by the Tractarians. Partly as a consequence of these seating arrangements though not only for this reason, men and women often took communion separately. At Swanage the twelve oldest men of the congregation communicated first. (A more normal order of precedence was, of course, by social class.) The medieval Housel cloth was perhaps the distant origin of the old custom of placing a clean handkerchief on the altar rails before communicating. There was also an insistence that the offering at the sacrament service ought to be of silver. None of these things was ordained by the Church but all were authentic popular customs which reveal the existence of religious traditions and usages distinct from those of the official doctrine. In one striking instance popular religion seems to have called into being a ceremony quite unknown to statute or canon law but which will not be unfamiliar to students of anthropology. Ruth Tongue (**84**, pp. 148–9) records a tradition of a legitimising ceremony performed in front of the parson in the parish church: 'And that gurt beardy man he do croopy on hands and knees and she do pull the hem of her Sunday black over him and Parson do say the words to right'n so he should aget farm.' A better known popular belief about the powers of the Church was that the parson could authorise the killing of aged parents who had become a burden and that the Church even provided a special club or 'church mawle' for this purpose (**65**, pp. 96–8; **63**, pp. 19, 127.)

The belief in the strange powers of the Established Church extended beyond the ranks of its own members. It was not only what Baxter called 'the healing custom' of occasional conformity or the established practice of marriage or burial by the Established Church even though the family involved normally worshipped at a meeting house that demonstrates this recognition, but also the fact that Dissenters, too, practised the same folkrites as the nominal Anglican. Henderson (**19**) records the case of a Baptist minister's son carrying out the church porch watch for the dead of the coming year. We hear of a Primitive Methodist asking a vicar for a shilling from his 'sacrament silver' because 'her child had fits and she had heard that if a sacrament piece of silver were hung around his neck it would cure him' (**21**, p. 300). A second case (*op. cit.*) concerns a Dissenter offering twelve pence for a 'sacrament shilling' with which to buy a ring which would cure a girl of fits. The Established Church and its rites thus seems to have had a practical power and utility even for those who could not or would not subscribe to its formal creed. There is, however, another side to the story. If the superstitious treated the clergy and their works with an exaggerated respect, the bold could be independent in the extreme. Consider this account of an interview between Parson Woodforde and a certain Harry Dunnel on 1 October, 1777. 'Harry Dunnel behaved very impertinently to me because I would not privately name his child for him, he having one child before named privately by me and never had it brought to church afterwards. He had the impudence to tell

21

me that he would send it to some Meeting House to be named etc.'
(**13**, p. 137). (See also **20**, p. 182 for a measure of the relative popularity of folk and church rites during Woodforde's incumbency.)

The history of popular anticlericalism in this country has yet to be written, perhaps because the materials so far accumulated have proved too meagre to bear the weight of a major study, but there can be no doubt that the question of tithes cause the most tension and indeed downright hostility between priest and people. Tithe exactions after a bad season could provoke riots as for example when the bishop was made to forgo his tithe of potatoes from the Isle of Man in 1825, and evading the tithe was like smuggling and poaching regarded by many as a kind of common law right. Folk-song asserted, 'We've cheated the Parson, we'll cheat him again', but equally folk speech had the phrase ' 'Tis sure as the thorn bush', alluding to the custom of marking every tenth stook—which would be collected by the tithe proctors—with a thorn twig. Folk art too documents this theme for us. The County Museum at Truro has a Staffordshire group dated *c.* 1825 and entitled 'The Tithe pig'. It shows the parson rubbing his hands in anticipation as an honest couple bring in their sheaves, their fruits, two piglets—and a baby. The point is made quite explicit by the verse on, for example, a Liverpool mug of the second half of the eighteenth century now in the Victoria and Albert Museum [**doc. 11**]. Sydney Smith [**doc. 9**] ironically sees 'decimation' as a major tenet of Anglicanism.

The tithe bore of course most heavily on Dissenters, and in Ireland it was a major social issue. The resentful Catholic peasant murdered or mutilated the tithe collectors and sometimes tithe-payers too, while the reviled Church of Ireland clergy starved. In 1831 the Archbishop of Dublin said, 'As for the continuance of the tithe system, it seems to me that it must be at the point of the bayonet—that it must be through a sort of chronic civil war' (**79**, iii, 25). Feeling in England never approached this. The English farmer, whether out of some vestigial belief or simply fearing the consequences of refusal, evaded and grumbled but paid.

The gentleman parson sometimes asserted his authority over the community in a second capacity—as magistrate and these clerical justices seem to have been regarded with peculiar dislike. The Hammonds (**31**, ch. XIII) write of the clerical magistrates' ardour and thoroughness 'that made the discontented look upon them as the most unpitying of justices'. As late as 1873 Jesse Collings, after the notorious Chipping Norton strike case in which sixteen women received sentences of hard labour for alleged intimidation, advised labourers that if they were ever brought before the magistrates they should try to choose the day, if they could, when there was no clergyman on the bench. Although he had lived all his life in the country, he had never known a lenient sentence, nor anything short of the rigour of the law, come from a clergyman (**82**, p. 59). The *Church Herald* however took the view that 'the two clerical magistrates who acted so properly deserve the hearty thanks of all order loving people' (11 June 1873). The character and record of clerical magistrates in this period would make an interesting theme for research. It could be that much of this 'rigour' reflected the dissenting sympathies of so many of the discontented. One recalls the words of George Loveless [**doc. 8**]. The relationship of the masses to their Church was a complex one. This too is a subject crying out for further investigation. One may discern strands of genuine respect, of 'in-group' feeling against outsiders, of superstitious veneration, of economic tension. There was rarely one overriding influence. When it comes to defining the ordinary parishioner's view we shall no doubt conclude that 'One man in his time plays many parts'.

If the attitudes of the masses towards their own Church are difficult to summarise, their views of minority bodies tended to be simpler. Dissenters might be regarded by enlightened clergy as 'separated brethren' [**doc. 7b**] and their theological difficulties might be accommodated. Tradition says, for example, that at Ravenstonedale (Westmorland) a bell was rung after the creed in order to call in Dissenters for the sermon. The common man, however, knew that Dissenters were different and ought to be frankly treated as such. It has even been suggested (**21**, p. 154) that certain north–south burials at e.g. Cowden (Kent) and Bergholt (Suffolk) are those of Dissenters. Traditional ideas as to likely events on the Day of Judgment had led to the practice of burial west–east for members of the congregation and east–west for a clergyman so he would rise facing his flock. In this connection we might note a recently collected example of an old story from Tregongeeves (Cwll) (*Sunday Times*, 31 August 1969). The local story was that Quakers 'have themselves buried upright so as to be quick off the mark on Judgment Day'. Quakers, like Dissenters in general were held to have more than their fair share of competitive instinct. The dying Quakers' ambiguous advice to his son is said to have been, 'Get

23

money honestly if thou canst'. Attitudes to Dissenters whether
Protestant or Catholic could be friendly ones based on daily fam-
iliarity or they could be distorted by traditional fear fantasies
unleashed in times of national crisis [**doc. 9b**]. When panic really
reigned even polar opposites would be confounded. In 1655 Prynne
had published a work entitled *The Quakers Unmasked and clearly
detected to be but the spawn of Romish frogs, Jesuit and Franciscan Friars
sent from Rome to seduce the intoxicated, giddy-headed English nation* (**1** ii,
155). Fear of the Catholics seems to have been a metropolitan rather
than a rural phenomenon. The slander of their responsibility for the
Great Fire is well known, and rumours of truly baroque splendour
were in circulation on the eve of 1780 Gordon Riots—bands of
Jesuits were hidden in tunnels awaiting the word from Rome to
blow up the banks of the Thames and flood London and monks
disguised as Irish chairmen were poisoning the city's flour supplies
(**75**, ch 2 for these and other examples). Even those great purveyors
of anti-papalism, the Methodists could be tarred with the same
brush, for Hogarth in his canvas 'Credulity'—a conspectus of
contemporary superstition and fanaticism—gives the Methodist
preacher a tonsure. Methodists also incurred other suspicions. Their
'love feasts' of prayer and biscuits and water simply could not be
believed in. Dark rumours of orgies circulated. In 1944 an old man of
the Cranbrook district in Kent passed on the tradition to me as
follows: 'There's a room behind the chapel and when they've had the
prayers and a bite to eat they turn down the gas and it's every man
for himself. They call it a love feast!' It is the same story as told in
the sixteenth century by Brantôme of the Huguenots in their
temples [**doc. 12**].

As for the Jews a story from Mayhew (**80**, p. 274) shows old medieval superstitions still alive and poisonous in the middle of the last
century.

A gentleman of my acquaintance was one evening about twilight,
walking down Brydges Street, Covent Garden, when an elderly
Jew preceding him, apparently on his return from a day's work
as an old clothes man. His bag accidentally touched the bonnet
of a dashing woman of the town, who was passing and she turned
round, abused the Jew and spat at him, saying with an oath:
'You old rags humbug! *You* can't do that!'—an allusion to the
vulgar nation that Jews have been unable to do more than
slobber, since spitting on the Saviour.

Part Two

THE CHURCH AND ITS RIVALS

5 The Church Aware

How far did the Church recognise and seek to remedy its own faults? This question to which we first address ourselves would seem to be a very natural starting point from which to begin our dynamic analysis of the Anglican Church. The period 1750 to 1850 can hardly avoid being seen as a trough between the sectarian earnestness of the seventeenth century and the great controversy of the apes and the angels that broke out in the middle of the nineteenth century. We can see it as a sluggish and inactive age. We ask ourselves whether what Gibbon called 'the fat slumbers of the Church' were ever disturbed by the sleeper's uneasy conscience. More than one consideration, however, will prompt us to suggest that the question, unless it is radically qualified, may in fact be an invalid one.

In the first place, did the Church ever see itself, in this period, as other than an aspect of society as a whole [**docs. 1, 2**]? Perhaps from the time of the Nonjurors to that of the Oxford Movement a 'Church centred' view was so unusual as to be a positive eccentricity and it was this view of Church and State as obverse/reverse of the same coin ('Whose is the image and the superscription?' Matthew 22:20) that identified any criticism of the Church with criticism of the very structure of society itself (and so conversely [**doc. 6c**]). Until the age of the French Revolution no alternative model of a social order really existed and radical social criticism was unknown in early Georgian society. A second consideration bearing on the validity of the question we ask is that the Church of England embraced such a diversity of viewpoints, High, Low and Broad parties themselves embracing subgroups and divergencies (**9**), that it is difficult to ascribe collective views on any but the broadest issues to the Church as a whole. Furthermore, the absence of Convocation during the period under review deprived the Church of any opportunity for issuing or even discussing programmes and policies. However, when all such allowances have been made and caveats entered, one cannot escape the fact that complacency seems to have been the commonest attitude of Anglicans towards their Church [**doc. 28**]. Nor was this complacency the satisfied feeling with which the British political constitution was regarded, it was more an acceptance of unavoidable inadequacies. After all, pocket boroughs were defended as providentially useful institutions whereas the unserved churches, the pluralities and the political involvement of the bishops were seen as the unavoidable consequence of a human situation. The eighteenth-century clergyman did not make great demands on God but many on the patience of his people.

This hopeless and essentially unspiritual attitude did not of course hold all in its grip. We must never forget that the Methodist movement came from within the Church itself and that this movement testifies to an awareness of the Church about its own inadequacies. (The ultimate rejection of the movement by the Church is also an index of some clergy's obtuseness and lack of perception.) The argument would seem to have been, 'We dislike Dissenters. Let us make more of them' [**doc. 13b**]. The Evangelical Movement too is a proof of a religious sensitivity within the Church though this movement, like that of the Methodists, was inclined to flow over the boundaries of the Establishment system. Finally, the Oxford Movement also postulates the existence of clergy and people who saw the need for a more spiritually active Church and thus expressed their discontent with the attitudes of what Newman condemned as the 'two bottle orthodox' (**56**). These three movements show that Churchmen were concerned about the state of the Church though they could not agree as to the objective remedies to be applied. The real urge to reform came from Parliament and it was this that shocked the Church into self-examination of the most radical kind. Nevertheless, the old complacency seems to have held its own remarkably well [**doc. 24**], and little if anything was learned from the Methodist schism. Consider its attitude to the navvies:

Altogether the Anglican Church did not cover itself in glory in its dealing with the navvies. In the early years the country clergy seem carefully to avoid having anything to do with them . . . the extent of many a country vicar's interest in the men was to send his curate along to bury a few of them every now and again . . . the navvy way of life was frequently condemned. The clergy would have done the same for any sinners. . . . Most of the missionaries and scripture readers were sent by the nonconformists' (**70**, pp. 169, 173).

Such complacency, such self-confidence should logically express itself in some degree of tolerance and charity or at worst indifference to those outside.

How tolerant was the Church of England to those who dissented from its articles of faith? The first half of the century saw some grisly examples of naked persecution when an unfortunate individual, not in himself very important in his sect, found himself trapped in the toils of the law. In 1729 Matthew Atkinson, a Catholic priest, died in Hurst Castle after thirty years' imprisonment. Woolston the Deist died in prison in 1733 being unable to raise the fine of £100 that would have secured him freedom. Daniel Holles, a Quaker, was in prison for fifty years (1709–58) and lost property to the value of £700, all for a tithe debt of a few shillings. Cases like these can be found later in our period but the victims then are more obviously not only technical Dissenters but also eccentrics. Richard Brothers and George Gordon are examples here. To the great Anglican majority the yoke of the Church of England was an easy one, as indeed in many ways it was. The corrollary of this view was that those who refused the yoke were at best perverse or at worst depraved. In any case to press differences of religious opinion to the point of personal discomfort, let alone martyrdom, proved the presence of the dreadful condition of 'enthusiasm', and when that charge was brought a hostile verdict could scarcely be avoided. The case of the Catholics and that of the Jews, both unpopular minorities quite unlikely to win any mass following, provide touchstones for Anglican attitudes. Because of their association with Jacobitism, the whole weight of the law was poised to push Catholics into conformity, the accepted symbol of loyalty to the regime. In practice, the harshest of these laws were never enforced, but the threat was always there and at the very least they made any kind of public life impossible and undoubtedly this consideration accounts for the 'conversion' of such noblemen as the eleventh Duke of Norfolk (24). Dr Johnson, a devout Anglican, touched the nerve of the situation when he said 'I think all Christians whether Papists of Protestants agree in the essential articles, and that their differences are trivial and rather political than religious.' Sectarian barriers were not dogmatically defended. Johnson was willing enough to sympathise with much Catholic teaching though he conceded the frequent unsoundness of Catholic practice. His well-known distinction between the elements of Fancy in religion 'which we may take for a companion' and those of Reason 'which we must take as our guide' would have been for many an apt summary of the differences between Rome and Canterbury. Cowper's Roman Catholic friend Throckmorton, who remarked to his chaplain on the absurdity of praying in Latin, surprised the poet by this sign of 'liberality and freedom from bigotry' (**72**, p. 263).

In the eighteenth century and early nineteenth the Catholic Church in England had no diocesan organisation and needed the protection of the laity rather than being able to take any initiative itself. The English Catholics, led by their committee of eleven under Lord Petre, were 'Cisalpine' or Gallican in outlook and the renegade Duke of Norfolk taunted them with following the same road to Protestantism, saying he had anticipated them by thirty-five years! (One can see logic in his view. The English translation of Gallican should be Anglican.) However, the Catholic Church was not being eroded in the way Church and State had hoped. It was even making some converts. The venerable Bishop Challoner (1691–1781) had come from a Sussex nonconformist family and such diverse personalities as James Boswell and Edward Gibbon had felt the spell of 'the Old Religion'. The law was now regularly interpreted in a sense favourable to toleration and from 1771 on Parliament gradually dismantled the system of Penal Laws. In 1789 Parliament began making the realistic distinction between 'Protesting Catholic Dissenters' and the sinister 'Papists' against whom the former laws had been directed. In 1829 the last general exclusion, from Parliament itself, was ended [**doc. 9**] illustrates the contradictions of the 'exclusionists']. Catholic emancipation was advocated on political not religious grounds, and with reference to Ireland rather than to England for, as Halévy has written, 'the influence of the Catholics of the United Kingdom on the intellectual life of the nation was slight, on the economic life even slighter'(**4**).

Like all immigrant communities, the Jews were often pointed at as a source of crime and poverty, and the conversion to Judaism of the eccentric Lord George Gordon made the Jews a topic for comment and ridicule. Public thinking on the Jews was always in terms of an unfavourable stereotype though it is as early as 1753 that Smollett (in *Ferdinand Count Fathom*) made, in depicting the character Joshua Manesseh, 'the first frank effort to do justice to the Jewish people in English literature!' In the 1780s the liberal Dissenter Joseph Priestley conducted a religious controversy with the Jewish scholar shoe-maker David Levi. The radical Cobbett was violently antisemitic. It was from the heart of the Establishment that there emerged a genuine champion of the cause of human understanding across the gulf of faiths. Richard Cumberland (1731–1811), dramatist and journalist, was the great-grandson of an English bishop and son of a rector who became a bishop of the Church of Ireland. He himself had been intended for the Church. In earlier plays, *The West Indian* and *The Fashionable Lover*, he had attempted the sympathetic presentation of Irish and Scots characters: now, in *The Jew* (1793), produced at Drury Lane in 1794, he sought, through the character Sheva, to redress the damage done since Tudor times by the image of the vindictive Shylock. It cannot be said that Cumberland was entirely successful—Fagin was still to be born—and Cumberland himself said that not even the Jews appreciated his work. Nevertheless, it was a small victory for the cause of humanity and tolerance and indeed effective enough to call forth a protest from William Cobbett, a true spokesman of the masses whether for good or evil. Cobbett disliked the minor theatrical vogue for Jewish moralists that followed and said so vigorously (*Political Register*, 8 Oct. 1818).

Meanwhile, in 1809, a mixed group of Churchmen and Dissenters had formed 'The London Society for Promoting Christianity among the Jews' (**27**). The Society, reorganised in 1815 as an exclusively Church of England concern, was supported by many of the leading Evangelicals, including Wilberforce, Simeon, Ashley, Grimshaw and Bishop Ryder, but was often, as in 1825, the object of High Church attack (**25**, p. 77). By 1837 a community of converts had come into being and regular Hebrew worship with a translated Prayer Book had been established in London. By 1842 the Archbishop of Canterbury had become the Patron of the Society and most of the bishops vice-patrons. In the same year a convert of the Society was installed as the first Protestant Bishop of Jerusalem. 'Indeed the twenty years ending in 1850 may be considered the palmy years of the London Mission which then reached its highest level. The work of those years has never been surpassed' (**25**, p. 211). (See, however, Brontë, **67**, ch. 7 for reference to the 'Jew basket' and the trivial character of much 'activity' in this cause.) The Society, like many other Evangelical activities, struck no deep roots among the nominally Anglican masses. When people thought of the Jews at all it was in economic terms. To the rich they were bankers or bullion dealers (**62**, p. 190), to the poor they were old clothes men or pedlars.

In the 1830s, however, this general indifference was shaken by the Jewish Emancipation issue (**26**).

During this hard-fought struggle the Anglican Church had no one voice. Archbishop Whately of Dublin made a powerful plea for Jewish rights; Dr Arnold of Rugby revealed himself as equally strongly anti-Jewish and was rebuked from the House of Lords by Bishop Thirlwall. One of the leading opponents of the Jewish cause, despite his patronage of the London Society, was Bishop Samuel Wilberforce who in 1847 condemned the Jews as having 'no home . . . no hope . . . and hardly a God' (**2b**). The same theme was embroidered by T. R. Birks, Rector of Kelshall, in his *Letter to Lord John Russell* (1848), where he wrote of Jews as 'uncertain whether there be a revelation, a future judgment, a life to come, an Almighty and Holy government of the Universe'. It is true enough that the poor urban Jew was often grossly ignorant of the faith from which he took his name but probably no more so than the slum dwelling 'Christian' [**doc. 30**]. As was the case with the Catholics the achievement of emancipation was a political victory rather than one for theological dialogue. A religiously plural society was increasingly accepted as inevitable if not actually desirable. Many Jews gained a new self-confidence and revived their ancient faith, while others, perhaps now the more consciously eccentric, still joined the Church of England. Joseph Wolff (1795–1862) was one such (**78**). Son of a Bavarian rabbi, he in due course made his pilgrimage to Canterbury. He became curate of High Hoyland (Yorks) married a Lady Georgiana Walpole, went on a perilous adventure to Central Asia but died in rural peace as incumbent of Ile Brewers in Somerset. A more complete integration into the ecclesiastical and social establishment can hardly be imagined.

6 The Impact of Methodism

'Sir, the pretending to extraordinary revelations and gifts of the
Holy Ghost is a horrid thing—a very horrid thing.' Bishop Butler to
John Wesley (**29**, p. 75). 'Begging your honour's pardon, may not
the new light of God's grace shine upon the poor and ignorant in
their humility, as well as upon the wealthy and the philosopher in all
his pride of human learning?' Humphry Clinker to Squire Bramble
(**83**).

Methodism is the subject of a vast literature and although it has
devoted to it a separate volume in this Seminar Studies series (**28**)
it also claims its place in our study of the Established Church
and popular religion. The nature, impact and significance of the
Methodist movement are still matters of lively controversy (**17**) (**29**)
(**35**). Interpretations may be theological or social (variant names
for the subjective and objective?); the movement may be assessed
as benign by Wearmouth (**36**) or as positively malignant as by
Plumb (**35**) or Thompson (**17**). Its significance may well have been
exaggerated (as argued on the political front by Hobsbawn (**38**) but
it was a movement that mirrored its times and perhaps can still
illuminate our own. Our interest here must be in Methodism's
ambiguous association with the Establishment and in its other
character as an aspect of popular religion.

Let us first of all look at Methodism through the eyes of its founder,
John Wesley, writing to the Bishop of Lincoln in 1790 [**doc. 13b**].
'The Methodists in general . . . are members of the Church of
England. They hold all her doctrines, attend her service, and
partake of her sacraments. . . . To encourage each other . . . they
frequently spend an hour together in prayer and mutual exhortation.'
Certainly it was always Wesley's intention that this should be the
case, though when one considers the 356 chapels in virtually church-
less places, the tightly organised structure of class, band and society
and the fact that as early as 1760 ' . . . Methodism was easily the
most highly coordinated body of opinion in the country, the most

33

fervent, the most dynamic!' (**35**) it is difficult to see these facts reflected in Wesley's ingenuously modest words. Wesley may well have deceived himself as to the total compatibility of the Church of England and his host of noisy fuglemen but we would be equally wrong to overstress their disharmony. By 1750 when the period under our review opens, the old crude hostility to the Methodists had largely died down, though not before talk of inevitable secession had begun. A century later when our period closes we see the Wesleyans forced into technical dissent, rent by internal controversy, assailed by the Tractarians and about to begin yet another retreat from their founder's Tory ideal. This period, the heroic age of Methodism, embraces the life span of Robert Newton (1780–1854) whose biography (**33**) was written by Thomas Jackson, Methodist champion in the clash with the Puseyites. Newton was a Wesleyan minister of international reputation, great eminence and unimpeachable orthodoxy. He lived and died a pillar of his church. His biography has much to say on Anglican–Methodist relations, and to see this evidence assembled in so late a document (the biography was published in 1855) is to gain new insights into the question.

Robert Newton, as was the case with so many Methodists, was no lost soul dragged from the brothel or the drinking den. His parents, farmers of Roxby in Yorkshire, were Church attenders and communicants who, in the true Wesleyan spirit added Methodism to their regular religious practices. Robert, when aged eleven, was sent to Whitby for confirmation by the Archbishop of York, in 1791. After a copybook conversion at the age of eighteen, he began to preach and was eventually ordained to the full ministry. He subsequently found a wife from an Anglican family of Skelton. She 'had been awakened to a concern for her salvation under the ministry of pious clergymen of the Church of England of which she was a member'. In 1803 Newton began his long association in the cause of foreign missions, with Dr Coke 'a clergyman of the Church of England, hearty in his attachment to Methodism'. A relation of his wife suggested to Newton that he should formally transfer his ministry to the Established Church and even offered to provide a church for him. The invitation was politely declined. In 1812 he moved to the capital where 'in most of the London chapels he found the Liturgy of the Church of England used in the forenoon of every Lord's Day. To him this was a novelty but no inconvenience. . . . At this period he contracted such a love for the Liturgy, that in future life it afforded him sincere satisfaction to be appointed to circuits where the people were accustomed to the use of it.' Finally Newton's biographer rehearses his view of the true state of relationship between the Methodists and the Anglicans.

As a religious community [the Methodists] have never declared their hostility to the Church as a national establishment, nor have they ever affected to interfere with the revenues of the Clergy, or the prerogative of the Crown in the bestowal of ecclesiastical preferment. Many members of the Methodist Societies attend the services of the Church and receive the Lord's Supper at her altars. The two Wesleys lived and died in her communion; Sellon and Fletcher, the very able and earnest defenders of the Wesleyan theology were of her Clergy; so was Dr Coke, the father of the Wesleyan Missions; and so were Messrs Richardson, Dickenson, and Creighton who were officially connected with the Methodist chapels in London (**33**, p. 139).

One might add that Newton's whole life is a testimony to the viability of Wesley's wish for committed Methodist and cautious Anglican to be fellow workers in the same vineyard. Here we perhaps overstressed the antagonism between Methodism and the Established Church? The relationship was a complex one which has not yet been exhaustively analysed, the complexity and regional variations arising directly from the fact that the Church in the Erastian Age was allowed no independent voice. We find then Methodist and Anglican in every possible degree of interdependence and antagonism. Paradox would appear to be the rule. If the Wesleyans of Tolpuddle were classed as Dissenters [**doc. 8**] on the one hand, then on the other we may cite such a man as Thomas Bateman (1799–1897), twice President of the Primitive Methodist Conference, who '. . . all his life retained some connection with the Established Church' (**81**, p. 180).

What were the forces then that led to the ejection of the Methodists from the Church whose stay and strength they might have been or, to borrow a sentence from Dr Wearmouth (**27**), embodying a more conciliatory attitude—what forces led to the 'creation and unfolding of a new religious denomination whose parentage and birth were in the Established Church'? Firstly we must name the internal contradictions of Wesley's own position: faithful to the discipline

35

of the Established Church in all things except on the crucial points of 'Who is a bishop?' and 'Who is entitled to ordain?' Secondly we must name the bishops and magistrates who 'bent' the terms of the Toleration Act to force Methodists into accepting the legal status of Dissenters. This is the gravamen of Wesley's plea to Bishop Tomline [**doc. 14**]. R. E. Davies (**29**), chap. 6 admirably summarises the position: 'The authorities of the Church of England did precisely nothing, either to prevent a breach or to expel the Methodists. Individual bishops from time to time acted in their own diocese in ways that showed they approved or disapproved of what the Methodists were doing. But of concerted action there was nothing.' Methodism was an embarrassment and a living reproach to the Church. Many Anglicans were undoubtedly relieved when the movement's own momentum changed it from a satellite of Canterbury into some sort of planet in its own right. Once classed as Dissenters, however reluctantly, the Methodists automatically fell under the same social condemnation as other outsiders. A third factor to be considered was of course the fact that the Methodist revival was not and could not be confined to the ranks of even nominal Anglicans. It swept over all the separate fragments of the divided Christian Church. This would-be exclusively Anglican movement therefore swept in many people of Dissenting origin who inevitably assisted the trend towards schism.

These last considerations logically bring us to the question 'Who were the Methodists?' E. P. Thompson's complaint (**17**, p. 918) that 'too much writing about the Methodists commences with the assumption that we all know what Methodism was', is a very valid one. There is some evidence to suggest that Methodists themselves made certain false assumptions or, shall we say, too easily confused their aspirations with their achievements. Let us start with Wesley himself, suggesting as he does [**doc. 13**] that the ranks of the drunkards, swearers and harlots made significant contributions to the swelling numbers of the Methodists. We find the same sentiment in Jackson's biography of Newton cited above: 'The Founder . . . and his fellow labourers . . . waited not till ignorant multitudes should apply to them for instruction. . . . They rather forced an entrance into neighbourhoods where wickedness abounded, warning the people of danger. . . .' (**33**, p. 2). It may well be that at certain times and in certain places there was some truth in this but the scene can also be shown in a different light. Let us for example consider the advent of Methodism to the Easingwold Circuit of Yorkshire as recorded in *Memorials of Early Methodism* (**30**). Methodist preachers were first invited to Easingwold itself by 'officials of the National Church', the parish clerk and sexton. There was mob violence, and the local authorities were of no assistance. The Thirsk magistrate, however, intervened and serious disturbance ceased. Wesley visited Easingwold several times and in 1786 preached in 'the new house' there. At about this time John Crosby of Whitby began to preach in the area. He had been converted to active Christianity by the vicar of Pickering but had eventually joined the Methodists. How he discovered his gift for preaching is the subject of an anecdote which epitomises the whole ethos of Methodism [**doc. 14**]. The Helmsley society owed its foundation to the removal of Dr Conyers, the minister there, a man of Calvinistic tendencies. When he left the village 'those who had been awakened could only find spiritual help and guidance among the Methodists'. The advent of Methodism to Hawnby is perhaps best described in the words of our source.

> Two men were at work in the neighbourhood, and being over-come with heat and fatigue, they lay down by the side of the hedge and fell asleep. They dreamed they were not fit to die and appear before God, and were much affected by the deep and painful sense of guilt produced on their minds by the Holy Spirit. . . . One of them applied to a clergyman, who told him that his was a case of religious melancholy and that . . . he should go into company and strive to enjoy himself. . . . By the good providence of God, a newspaper fell into their hands containing an advertisement that . . . Mr Wesley intended to preach at Newcastle . . . a few like-minded went to hear that truly apostolic man.

The case of Elizabeth Hodgson who first invited Methodists to Raskelf also has its points of interest.

> Her parents regularly attended the services of the Established Church, and taught her in early life to pray to God and repeat the Church catechism . . . from her general stability, the correctness of her morals, and her uniform attention to public and private religious duties, she was deemed a Methodist by her neighbours, thought it does not appear that at that time she had any acquaintance with the Methodist Society.

37

Methodism came to Hutton Sessay through the agency of a retired surgeon and to Kilburn through Mrs. Lawns who owned the bakehouse. The list of the original trustees of Crayke Chapel (1787) shows them to be all tradesmen or yeomen. There is little in these narratives to suggest any one forcing an entrance into areas where wickedness abounded. How different was the situation elsewhere? There is ample scope here for detailed local research.

There is reason also to believe that the reputation of Methodism often bulked larger than its membership would justify. Consider this firsthand account quoted in our source (**30**): 'It was said about this time [1797] that all Husthwaite had turned Methodists, with many ridiculous tales about them. I rode past the place one day, and saw a man sowing, and looked hard at him to see what he was like, for I thought he would be a Husthwaite man and most likely a Methodist.' In fact, over the next twenty years the village seems to have had no more than half a dozen Methodists in it. As one reads through these simple annals the same points are reiterated. Methodists were objects of hostility at first and then of mere curiosity. They were not the poorest of the poor and came for the most part from religious backgrounds. Hannah Harrison was the daughter of a Presbyterian brewer, George Tyndale of Brandsby came from an actively Anglican family, John Atlay of Sheriff Hutton 'used to go to the Sacrament at all opportunities' from the time he was sixteen years old. Thomas Mitchell was converted by Grimshaw, the Vicar of Haworth. William Carlton of Sutton was born to parents who 'attended the parish church regularly and to the best of their knowledge trained up their children in the fear of God'. Carlton underwent a conversion at the age of fifteen and attached himself to a Methodist congregation. The only manifest 'sinner saved' yielded by these pages is the Rev. Thomas Vasey who came himself from a Methodist home. Self-confessed as 'one of the wickedest wretches in the village' before he was twelve, his depravity led him so far as quarrelling with his brothers and playing on the Sabbath. His salvation began at the age of fifteen after a horrifying dream of universal destruction. There is little doubt that in the Easingwold Circuit, which we have no reason to believe was untypical, Methodism was a religious revival that began—and largely ended—among those already under the influence of the church but who sought experiences of more satisfying intensities. Their number was always small and their impact on the social structure negligible.

To what extent if at all can Methodism be seen as 'popular religion'? Plumb's downright verdict 'not of the poor but for the poor' (**35**) has much obvious justification besides stating succinctly much that is rehearsed at great length by E. P. Thompson (**17**). Certainly there is no trace of 'nativism' in the Methodist cult, no defence or revival of popular beliefs in the face of alien domination indeed, to the contrary, 'The Wesleyans first, and the Primitive Methodists after them, repeatedly sought for outright confrontation with the older, half pagan popular culture. . . .' This is the testimony of G. Home in his study of Pickering, Yorks (**76**). Speaking of local tradition and custom he writes: 'There can be little doubt that the deathblow to this mass of ignorant superstition came with the religious revival brought about by the Methodists. . . . This change took place between about 1800 and 1840, but the influences that lay behind it go back to John Wesley' (p. 221).

All this is true enough as far as it goes but we may perhaps make a parallel with Wesley's political attitudes. He was a Tory and equated social Toryism with scriptural holiness. He simply could not impose the same yoking of concepts upon his followers [**doc. 15a**]. Perhaps this was also the case with popular religious (or superstitious) attitudes. Davies (**29**) who so rightly stresses the orthodoxy of Methodism also asserts the essential rationality of Wesley's approach. On the other hand Wearmouth (**36**) in two pages documenting rural superstition in Wesley's age seems to be advancing the idea that the credulity of the people made them more avid hearers of Wesley's preaching. Plumb (**35**) stresses that 'Wesley's superstitions were those of his uneducated audiences', and that 'everywhere in early Methodism one meets the prejudices of the uneducated'. Young Samuel Bamford, though his father was 'a burning and a shining light' among the Methodists, was well acquainted with the whole range of the popular custom and superstition of the Middleton area (**64**). In Henderson's folklore classic (**19**) it is true that we find a Methodist bride refusing to sanction the traditional race for one of her ribbons but we equally find the Methodist dressmaker warning a less well informed woman that the Saviour had cursed all who washed on Good Friday and telling the medieval story that explained this belief. The death of a Primitive preacher in West Riding was presaged by traditional omens despite his 'new birth'. The medieval and apocryphal *Letter to Abgarus* was, it seems, circulated in a version that incorporated Methodist hymns! Syncretism is a normal feature of popular religion and there is no reason to suppose that the early Methodists did not practise it. The first 'travelling preacher' of the Primitive Methodists was James Crawfoot of Delamere, the 'Old Man of the Forest'. He was suspected by some of the practice of magical arts. Hugh Bourne sat at his feet, heard his preaching and then paid him ten shillings a week to become a travelling evangelist.

The annals of Methodism are full of belief that at long last the heavens were open again and that God was speaking to man through dream and vision. Why should 'the new light of God's grace' not 'shine upon the poor and ignorant in their humility'? Until Humphry Clinker received the substantial consolation of being acknowledged as the squire's son, he was only too willing to console himself with the faith that he was a child of God.

7 Sectarian Movements

I met . . . an Anglican minister who, when I asked him how many sects there were in England replied: 'Sir, no one can say for certain, for every week some die out and fresh ones arise. It is enough if a man, whether he be of good faith or merely desirous of making a name and a fortune, instate himself in a good position where he can preach. He is immediately surrounded by a crowd. He explains some passage in the Bible in his own fashion, and if he pleases the people they invite him to preach again the following Sunday, generally at some tavern. He declaims his doctrines with energy, gets talked about, his adherents augment in proportion to his popularity; they take to themselves a name, and a sect is formed which the Government ignores until it begins to have political influence. Casanova (**68**, 189–90).

A Church is 'the institutional expression of a system of religious beliefs'. It is open to all and theoretically contemplates the inclusion of all the population as members. A Church is usually in significant relationship to the other major institutions of the society in which it operates. One is born into a Church rather than formally converted to its doctrines. The Church of England perfectly exemplifies all these characteristics. A sect on the other hand is characteristically, a small or limited organisation claiming to make available to a chosen few some exclusively held doctrine. It does not usually contemplate, even in theory, the 'capture' of the majority and their social system, but is rather in the nature of a secession. In some cases (the contemporary Jehovah's Witnesses sect is an example) there is actually a numerical limit set to full participation. From one point of view, sectarianism is the logical consequence of certain basic ideas of Protestantism. Grant that all necessary religious truths are contained in the Bible where any layman may find them for himself; deny the need for any interpreting authority or trained commentators and it is inevitable that a mass of divergent teachings will result. The first centuries of the Christian Church were a kaleidoscope of shifting theologies which gradually settled into the mainstream orthodoxies of Rome and Constantinople. The Middle Ages saw free interpretations of Scripture branded as heresy and in the main a monolithic conception of the Church was the normally accepted one. When the dams broke in the turmoil of the Reformation, 'do it yourself' theology was in vogue again and sects proliferated. In England the Civil War was a further stimulus to sectarianism. Up to our present century at least, the Church has been the seismograph of society. The fall of the Roman Empire, the end of the Middle Ages, the downfall of Divine Right monarchy, all these were preceded by rifts and ruptures in the religious establishment and the link between religious and political dissent was obvious to those closest to the seats of power. The theologian may see in the breaking away of numerous new sects the result of the action of the Holy Spirit. The historian is more inclined to consider them as at first reflecting (and later influencing) fundamental changes in the economic and social structures. It would be strange indeed if the age of the Industrial and French Revolutions did not have a disturbing effect on the traditional faith. To this extent—and also because they tended to draw their membership from the less sophisticated—the sects active in the period 1750 to 1850 must come under consideration in our study of popular religion.

They have, however, another claim as well. The man who begins a sect is perhaps doing no more than indulging his private fantasy, but if he finds a significant number of followers, and if moreover the sect survives the death of its founder, then we may infer that the movement satisfied some genuine hunger and can therefore be seen as an embodied criticism of the Established Church. Should sects of separate foundation persistently reproduce similar features, then a gulf plainly exists between the Established pastor and his flock. The Roman Church sometimes met this challenge with suppression, sometimes with the institution of a new devotion or the recognition of a new Order. The Anglican Church sometimes trimmed its sails in recognition of the new breeze (e.g. Evangelicalism as a response to the challenge of Methodism) or more often tuttutted and ascribed the movement to the work of agitators. Just as the medieval heresies usually overstressed one aspect of orthodoxy, so the English sect often points out an inadequacy of the Established Church.

A good example of the minimally significant, even grotesque, sectarian body is provided by the Muggletonians, yet even they have a proven life of two centuries and their little revivals suggest some significant correlation with periods of disturbance in the 'outside' world. Lodowick Muggleton, a London tailor, had been born in Bishopsgate Street in 1609. In 1651 he, with his cousin John Reeve, claimed to be the 'Two Witnesses' of Revelation 11:3. In the following year he published his *Transcendent Spiritual Treatise* and in 1656 *The Divine Looking Glass*. Muggleton lived on until 1698 despite not only the early death of his fellow witness and imprisonment and fines for blasphemy but also two separate repudiations by his own disciples. Sixty years later (1756) as the Seven Years' War engulfed Europe the Muggleton/Reeve works were republished and supplemented by *The Acts of the Witnesses*. In 1832 a new three-volume edition of the *Works* came out, though only sixty copies seem to have been subscribed for. In 1846 *The Divine Looking Glass* was reprinted by the dwindling group, but as late as 1902 a Muggletonian congregation is said to have been meeting in secret in the Bishopsgate district where the sect had had its beginning. The story of this strange body, quietly surviving in its corner of the busy City, illustrates the extreme tenacity of the sectarian impulse which, while entailing on the one hand social rejection and ridicule, also provided colour for drab lives and gave the humble satisfying illusions of spiritual grandeur.

One of the major sectarian figures of our period was Joanna Southcott (1750–1814), 'the Exeter Prophetess', a servant girl who successfully established 'Southcottian' churches in London, Birmingham, Bristol and many cities of the North, and who, though failing to give birth to the new Messiah as she promised, nevertheless became the prolific mother of sects even more eccentric than her own which, incidentally, still survives. The outward facts of her career are not in dispute. Daughter of a West Country farmer, she went into service with an Exeter tradesman's family and in 1792 casually announced her call as a prophetess while clearing the breakfast table. Gradually she acquired local fame with predictions about such things as movements of corn prices and the prospects of the harvest. She favoured the sealed, written prophecy in order to provide visible proofs of her powers but cynics asserted that her writing was so bad as to be only intelligible to herself! (**40**, p 54). This habit developed into a major characteristic of Joanna's

43

activity. She was constantly appealing for recognition and vindication from the established religious authorities, always offering herself—though very much on her own terms—for tests, trials and challenges. The Exeter Cathedral Chapter was one of the first bodies she approached in this way. A small inner group of disciples which included three Anglican clergymen and was known as 'the Seven Stars' came into being and the practice of 'sealing' believers was begun. Joanna gave the faithful slips of paper declaring them to be 'sealed of the Lord, the Elect Precious'. Perhaps as many as 100,000 people were enrolled in this fashion, though the tide was stemmed when one of the 'sealed' was hanged for murder.

Meanwhile Joanna moved to London from Exeter and her movement became a national rather than a regional one. The general drift of her teaching may be gathered from the titles of her now published prophecies; *The Strange Effects of Faith, A Dispute between the Woman and the Powers of Darkness* and *The Book of Wonders*. Apart from their veneration of one who claimed powers of prophecy, the Southcottians offered a supplement to orthodox theology. While asserting their genuine adherence to the Church of England and using its Prayer Book at their services, the Southcottians urged Joanna's claim to be a female Saviour who by a successful defiance of the Devil would reverse and obliterate the effects of Eve's sin in Eden. It was a theological 'Vindication of the Rights of Woman'. Nor was Joanna the only contemporary advocate of such a point of view. 'Mother' Ann Lee (1736–84) had taken theological feminism from England to America in 1774, proclaiming the bisexuality of God and her own role as a feminine counterpart of Christ whose coming inaugurated a new age of perfection. Ann Lee's preaching led to the establishment in the U.S.A. of a chain of 'Shaker' settlements, separatist, celibate and communist. In Scotland Elspeth 'Luckie' Buchan (1738–91) preached a similar gospel claiming to be 'the woman clothed with the sun' of Revelation 13 (**41**). 'Mother' Buchan incarnated the Spirit of God and promised to abide with the faithful until they ascended to Heaven at the end of the age. The existence of three contemporaneous feminine 'incarnations' in an age when the secular movement for women's rights was being inaugurated by Mary Wollstonecraft (1759–97) cannot be without significance. Here was a vast suppressed class that was at last finding advocates of its cause. The religious seismograph was reporting deep disturbances that led to major social movements later in the nineteenth century. (Women were a major element among the supporters of the antislavery movement and one of the strengths of Methodism was its utilisation of women, thus gaining access to human resources denied to the Church of England by its own masculine ethos).

Joanna's career now entered its last tragic phase. Bitterly criticised, not only by orthodox clergy but also by rival prophets, she made an attempt to stage a decisive 'trial' at Neckinger House, Bermondsey, in 1804. The nation was not convinced, though she still wistfully hoped that the bishops might assemble to examine and accept her claim. For ten years the stream of her rambling prophecies flowed on unabated. Perhaps the very dullness of it all forced her into making her last desperate bid for recognition and to prove that faith could achieve all things. She announced that in the sixty-fifth year of her age she would bear a Saviour child 'Almighty Shiloh' 'by the power of the Most High'. In December 1814 the elderly prophetess died. Disciples kept the body warm for some days in hope of a return to life. Her faith had indeed managed to produce the apparent signs of pregnancy but that was all. The faith of many of the disciples suffered a mortal blow, though successor prophets, George Turner, John Ward and John Wroe, managed to keep some remnants together. The Southcottians still maintain some sort of tenuous existence but the mass movement of 'Joannas' as they were popularly known was extinct by the mid-century.

The interest of the Joanna Southcott movement for our study may be summed up as follows: it is undoubtedly a religious movement of the people; while Joanna was alive it was not at all hostile to the Established Church though after her death John 'Zion' Ward reverted to Dissenting attitudes and condemned the Anglican clergy as 'false prophets'. Joanna's hopes of clerical sympathy were, of course, in vain. If the scholarly and capable John Wesley could not impress the bishops with his case, what hope was there for the humble Joanna with her deviant theology and rambling verse? Lastly in so far as it was a 'feminist' movement it was an implied criticism of orthodoxy by the common people. It was the only sectarian movement (apart from the ambiguous case of Methodism) that desired recognition by the Established Church. This fact is the best proof of Joanna's sincerity—and simplicity.

After Joanna Southcott the most considerable sectarian figure of our period was Richard Brothers (1757–1824). Born in Newfoundland, he entered the navy at an early age and saw service in the War of American Independence. Retired on half pay after the war he seems to have drifted into Quaker circles, and we next hear of him voicing conscientious objections to the periodic oaths required of him when he drew his pension. These scruples led him first into the hands of the Poor Law authorities and then to Newgate Prison for arrears of rent. On his discharge he resolved to leave London and had actually begun to do so when, like some latterday Dick Whittington, he heard a call that made him retrace his steps to the capital. God, he firmly believed, had chosen him as his prophet and would reveal to him a gospel for the age. The revelation was published in 1794, *A Revealed Knowledge of the Prophecies and Times, Wrote under the Direction of the Lord God.* The core of the message was simple enough: the end of the age was at hand, the Hebrews were to return in triumph to their Promised Land, Brothers himself was their Prince and Revelator, the war against France was in direct contravention of the Will of God. All this to the student of the sectarianism is familiar, indeed predictable stuff. Brothers backed his claim to be in the confidence of the Almighty by alleging he had twice already saved London from its merited destruction. The proof of his power was the continued existence of the capital! Brothers's denunciation of the war and his prediction of the overthrow of most of the established dynasties was heard with much satisfaction by members of the artisan and tradesman class, which seems to have been the source of the main body of his adherents. Some indiscreet words at the end of his book (where George III was warned to be ready to surrender his crown to the revealed Prince of the Hebrews) led to a discussion of treason charges and suspicion that Brothers was a Jacobin. He had in fact no significant radical associations though the artist William Sharp who engraved his likeness was a link between the Brothers–Southcott world and that more solid one of Tom Paine and Horne Tooke. The treason charge was not proceeded with, for Brothers was found to be insane. The prophesied date for the end of the age and assembling of the Hebrews in Jerusalem came and went. Brothers lived on, a discredited figure, lost in plans and specifications for the buildings of the capital city of the Hebrews. A few wealthy supporters fed his delusions. He died in 1824.

The Brothers movement in its original form was a transitory thing. He briefly caught the public imagination but was too precise (because too honest) in his predictions. He left himself no escape clauses such as are the badge of the imposter. He did, however, leave a strange inheritance to the generations that followed; the identification of the English with the true Israel. This doctrine not surprisingly made its first appearance under the Commonwealth among the sect called the Ranters (a name, incidentally, revived during our period and applied to certain Methodists) and in 1650 a certain John Robins was proclaimed King of Israel and expected to lead the Jews back to Jerusalem. The similarity to the teaching of Brothers is most striking. The whole ethos of Commonwealth Puritanism might be considered as leading up to such a revelation for the story of the lost tribes provided a logical means of harmonising the ideas of a spiritual and a physical 'Israel'. The Commonwealth, too, was a time of increased sympathy for the Jews, albeit in limited circles only. The 1780s and 1790s were also a time of increased sympathy for and understanding of Judaism. Brothers must have been in Newgate at the same time as Lord George Gordon, a distinguished convert to that faith. In the 1790s, as in the 1650s, ancient thrones were tottering, the social order was in chaos; to envisage the end of the age in terms of the imagery of the Apocalypse was a most natural thing for a Bible-reading generation. The doctrine that England was Israel survived Brothers and became a part of the broader Southcottian stream until it established itself as a movement in its own right. The British Israel movement lost much of its impetus in the years after the 1914–18 war, and its rise and decline might well be seen as a theological side effect of the development of British imperialism.

The next figure in this line of popular 'messiahs' had nothing of Joanna's *sancta simplicitas*, nor even the melancholy charm of Brothers in his early days, but was a rank imposter who changed his name and title as often as his clothes—and he had a spectacular wardrobe! John Nichols Thom (1799–1838) alias Sir William Courtenay, alias Squire Thompson, alias Hassan Abdullah, alias Count Moses Rothschild, was the only cult leader of our period whose followers died for him, for 'our only True Messiah, King of the Jews' (yet another of his assumed titles) proclaimed the invulnerability of the faithful and led his followers in a clash with troops at Bossenden Wood near Canterbury (**40, 42**). He was shot dead. Although from one point of view Thom was simply deranged, from another he can be seen as a significant focus of influences. As a young man in Cornwall he was an admirer of Brothers and he reproduced that prophet's Quaker and Jewish interests. It was as Count Moses Rothschild that he made his first appearance in Canterbury in 1832. He claimed to have visited the East seeking recognition for his own divine mission from Hester Stanhope, who wove her own fantasies in Lebanon. Thom had (or claimed) some affiliation to the radical group known as the Spencean Philanthropists and when questions were asked about him in Parliament there was an attempt to present his 'insurrection' as essentially a protest against the new Poor Law. His is the only movement, too, that bears traces of 'Nativism' (**38**), the assertion of traditional values in the face of external assault. Between 1832 and 1838 Tom built up a following in and around Canterbury partly as a political vindicator of human rights and partly as the human vehicle of Christ's second coming. As his following grew he marched about the countryside with sword and trumpet and two banners, a rampant lion and a traditional symbol of food rioters, a loaf on a pole. He administered the sacrament in bread and water and accepted divine honours as saviour. A constable was sent to arrest him but was shot dead by the messiah himself. Matters were now moving to a climax. Troops were called out from Canterbury and the last clash took place at Bossenden Wood, Boughton. As Thom fell he managed to gasp out the words, 'I have Jesus in my heart'. Transportations, prison sentences and public statements of penitence cleared up the affair from a legal point of view.

No sect resulted from the activity of this messiah for he taught no distinctive doctrine. He was simply a man of compelling personality who, like Joseph Smith the Mormon, had the gift of persuading other men to dream his dreams. Nevertheless his power was real enough for the officiating clergy to omit any reference to the hope of resurrection in his funeral service. His brains were carried away in a top hat by the surgeon who performed the autopsy. An enterprising local man shaved his dog and sold the hair as curls of the saviour's beard. As late as 1940 his preserved heart was still in existence and his Lion banner was rumoured to be still in Canterbury in 1945. I have met descendants of his disciples. His real significance for our study is the area in which he operated. If extravagances like this could take place almost in the shadow of the Mother Church of England what might not be possible in remoter areas? As a near contemporary historian wrote: 'It was long before the clergy of Canterbury heard the last of this' (**79**). The 'Courtenay

Delusion', as it is called, shows how weak was the grip of the Established Church in the very country where its tradition was theoretically strongest.

In the year that the Canterbury Messiah died the sect of 'Peculiar
People' or Plumstead Peculiars was founded by William Bridges and
John Banyard (**41**). The essential and distinctive belief of this pre-
dominantly working-class body which has never spread far beyond
the Kent and Essex shores of the Thames Estuary was the rejection
of medical aid and reliance on prayer and anointings, the scriptural
basis for this being James 5:14. The very name of the body breathes
the spirit of sectarianism for, to the uninitiated, it seems the acme
of the absurd, but to the diligent Bible reader it is at once known as
having a scriptural reference (I Peter 2:9). a passage which empha-
sises the privileged separateness of true believers from the world. The
sect still survives but without its traditional name the former
Peculiars, being content to use the more inconspicuous though still
perfectly accurate name of Evangelical. It is a strange quirk of
popular nomenclature that caused the last well-known leader of this
humblest of Christian bodies William Heddle who died in 1949 at
the age of 101, to be known as the 'Bishop'.

Even the Peculiars were not the ultimate in sectarian withdrawal,
for in 1850 one of their number John Sirgood (1820–85) took himself
off preaching into Sussex and founded the equally strangely named
'Society of Dependents' which remained a small Sussex-based community nickamed 'Cokelers' (**41**). The sect still maintains a precar-
ious existence.

Mary Ann Girling (1828–86) was a Suffolk country woman,
originally a Methodist compelled by visions to assume the title of
'Mother' of a humble community of 'Children of God' rudely
nicknamed 'the Walworth Jumpers' on account of their ecstatic
jerkings (compare Quakers, Shakers, Holy Rollers). Before our
period closes H. J. Prince (1811–99) had founded the Somerset
community known as Agapemone, 'the Abode of Love' (**40**), by no
means a manifestation of popular religion but certainly one that
evolved from within the Established Church. The significant cases
of the Irvingites or Catholic Apostolic Church and that of the
'Plymouth' Brethren will be discussed in another context in the next
chapter.

To sum up the argument of this chapter; the development of
mainstream Anglicanism during our period was paralleled by a

veritable ferment of sectarianism which would repay detailed local study. Even without this we may assert there to have been vast unappeased spiritual cravings which would not be satisfied either by a prayer book diet or by Wesleyan Methodism, for that movement, too, experienced increasing fragmentation as a result of more and more members asserting their right to an organisational expression for their political or theological point of view. By 1850 the movement Wesley had begun as Anglican, Tory and orthodox was Dissenting, liberalising and sectarian. A common core to all these sectarian movements is the implicit or explicit claim that grace and revelation are not to be confined to channels prescribed by law. Another persistent feature of this period in England is the 'feminist' element we have already noticed. In contrast to the sectarianism of the Reformation period and to some American extravagances English sectarianism of this time shows virtually no communist tendencies nor much interest in new marriage patterns. From 1850 on secularism competes with the religious idiom and revolutionary mythologies supplied new rhetorical images for the man at odds with his age.

E. P. Thompson (**17**) has tried to postulate a relationship between overt political or social activity and (after the collapse of these efforts) sectarianism seen as 'the chiliasm of despair'. This is the best general theory yet advanced and will certainly be the centre of more discussion.

Should Methodism be classed as a sect or a church(**29**) ? Perhaps the decisive question must be the motives of the adherent or perhaps, to reword the same point, the satisfactions a new convert anticipated from his membership. The sectarian sees himself as boarding an ark as the waters are rising. The churchman takes his place in a community rooted in the past, anticipating a future and embracing the dead as well as the living. The sectarian builds flimsy platforms from which to rise to heaven (e.g. the Buchanites) (**41**) the churchman raises cathedrals. Soon the ecstatic, the ascetic, the hierarchical and the traditional impulses, all possible sources of sectarian fragmentation, were to find a new synthesis in the Oxford Movement.

8 Evangelicals and Jacobins

There is no question of the Evangelical revival which took place within the ranks of the Established Church at the time of the Methodist Secession being in any sense a movement of popular religion. Even more than Methodism it should be characterised as religion 'not of the poor, but for the poor'. Indeed if we look at Wilberforce, for example, through the eyes of William Cobbett, one may see in his work a major factor in the increasing trend towards the alienation of the masses from the State Church. To this extent the historian may note the Evangelicals as a moulding force in the development of popular religious attitudes. To the student of religion, the interest of the problem is rather different. He would prefer to consider the extent to which the movement was a genuinely disinterested response to the religious challenge of the age [**doc. 19**] (taken at its face value) and how far a rationalisation of a purely socio-political policy [**doc. 20**]? To which challenge was Wilberforce really sensitive? The call to save souls in peril or the fear of the consequences of the masses succumbing to Jacobinism? It is true that Wilberforce's conversion and the King's Proclamation against vice, etc., preceded the revolution but only after the revolution did the implementation of 'Proclamation' policies become socially significant. He was certainly willing enough to stress the purely pragmatic aspects of his theological convictions [**doc. 18, a, d**]. Cobbett put the matter succinctly. The mission of the Saints, he said, was, 'to teach the people to starve without making a noise', and 'keeping the poor from cutting the throats of the rich'. His only consolation was that 'these fellows had no power over the mind of any but the miserable'. How far is this a just verdict?

Halévy (**4**, p. 56) saw the Evangelicals as the rearguard left behind by Wesley when he reluctantly broke with the Church of England, a rearguard still faithful to Wesley's original conception of a regenerating revival within the bounds of the Establishment. It was, however, not merely a question of clergy who had helped the

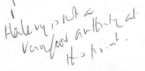

Halévy point is not
Various an attributed
to point.

51

Wesleyans continuing along these lines but of a new, selfconscious tendency with definite centres of influence and channels of communication. The new movement began at Cambridge with the ministry of Charles Simeon (1759–1836), the vicar of Christ Church, a gentleman of independent means who took no stipend. He gathered round him a 'remnant' organised in small groups—as the earlier Methodists had been—and he was the centre of a 'circuit' of parishes run on approved lines. He was a Wesley operating from a strong home base rather than conducting a guerrilla campaign. One might however note a new tendency. Simeon did not hesitate to invoke the law against his antagonists. This was something of a characteristic of Evangelicalism.

The other major focus was at Clapham, a London suburb, for more than ten years the home of William Wilberforce (1759–1833). At his home, bankers and lawyers, officials and men of independent means, laymen and clergymen, Anglicans and Dissenters, regularly met and brought into being an Evangelical 'platform' that crossed the boundaries of the Establishment at many points while always remaining firmly attached to it. 'A little party of their own, filled with self importance', is the slighting verdict of Halevy (4, p. 59). In doctrine the group avoided theological niceties, seeing themselves as Bible Christians by which they seem to have meant a moderate Calvinism. Certainly they saw Christians as a natural minority, albeit a leaven for the lump, and they saw the most trivial actions against the strong light of eternity. As a movement they found little support from the bishops, though Porteous of London (d. 1810) and Yorke of Ely (d. 1811) had some sympathy. In 1815 one of their own circle, Dr Ryder, was made Bishop of Gloucester, but it was a lonely triumph. Evangelicals were active in the establishment of proprietary chapels, in attacking the abuses of non-residence, in stimulating foreign missions, in distributing Bibles, in endeavouring to convert the Jews (25, 26). They attacked cruel sports, duelling, certain aspects of child labour and above all slavery. The rigid observance of the Sabbath was a tenet of the sect and the sight of Louis XVIII starting on his return to France on a Sunday excited in Wilberforce an eloquent grief that surely merited a grander cause. They were concerned with questions of crime and punishment, and thought the most profitable approach was to repress any and every manifestation of what Wilberforce called 'the general spirit of licentiousness which is the parent of every species of vice' (Diary

12 June 1787) and to fix the gaze of working people firmly on the goal of eternal life [**doc. 18c**]. It was all, Wilberforce thought, a matter of perspective and priorities for the masses and an eye to their obvious interests for the masters.

Time and time again the question of class intrudes into any discussion of the aims and methods of the Evangelicals (**31**, ch. 11 *passim*; **46**). The point seemed obvious to Cobbett and in 1802 Sydney Smith had also seized upon it, suggesting that Wilberforce's Society for the Suppression of Vice should properly have as an addition to its name the words 'among persons with less than £500 a year'. What then was the Evangelical policy towards the common man and his religious needs? Firstly, more churches with cheap or free accommodation [**doc. 19**] and by a Church Building Act of 1818 a million pounds was voted by Parliament for this purpose.* In addition the Evangelicals wanted more clergy, more prosecutions, more gratitude and above all, more working men, remodelled as Hannah More's wayward Robert Reeves was, on the pattern of Philip's eunuch (**31**). What did Wilberforce achieve? Whatever he failed to do for the common man he certainly did something to the middle and upper classes. 'An earnestness, hitherto the monopoly of the dissenting groups outside the mainstream of English life, invaded governing circles and the Church of England' (**6**). The *Annual Register* of 1798 had noted an outward and visible sign of this new spirit. 'It was a wonder to the lower orders . . . to see the aventures of the churches filled with carriages.' There is little doubt that the immediate motivation of this new religiosity was fear of the tumbril and one is inevitably reminded of the words of Dr Johnson, here given a wider social application: 'Depend on it Sir, when a man knows he is to be hanged in a fortnight, it concentrates his mind wonderfully.' Here as ever in the Erastian Age the Church is used as an instrument of government. The Sunday schools taught little children that if they were bad they would have to be burnt in fire and brimstone (see quotations in **74**). This might give rise to reflection but did it every excite any love for the Christian gospel?

---

* The last large-scale building of churches had been under Anne's Act for Fifty New Churches in 1711 and was a positive assertion of the place accorded to their High Church Anglicanism by the new Tory government. The post-1818 building (the so-called Waterloo churches) was an attempt to gain as much social advantage for as little expenditure as possible and only produced what Pugin damned as a 'mass of paltry churches'. Little if anything of distinction was created. These were churches of prudence, not of soaring faith.

It is obvious that the salvation religion and moral rigour of the Evangelical revival, whether interpreted by Wesley or by Wilberforce, resembles more than a little the Puritanism of the seventeenth century. There is, however, a significant difference. 'The puritan ideal was reborn shorn of its political radicalism' (**35**). The same point is also made by Thompson when he contrasts 'the positive energy of Puritanism, the self-preserving retreat of Dissent'; or again, more dramatically, 'Puritanism—Dissent—Nonconformity: the decline collapses into a surrender. *Dissent* still carries the sound of resistance. . . . Nonconformity is self-effacing and apologetic: it asks to be left alone'(**17**). Evangelicalism, one might add to complete the ideological paradigm, grovels. Oliver Cromwell's attributed last prayer contains many phrases ('miserable and wretched creature', 'very unworthy', 'mean instrument', 'poor worm') that were to become the debased currency of the ostentatiously humble and the smugly pious, but in the heroic age of Puritanism their implications were very different. The Puritan warrior abased himself before God as a matter of logic, but when turned towards man exalted himself above the godless as a matter of fact. The sense of election, the 'being in Covenant through Grace', generated the zeal and audacity that overthrew an anointed king and established England's Commonwealth. What we must note here is the other half of the picture. If the puritan body had risen again as a mumbling Evangelical zombie, in the ranks of the Jacobins so execrated by Wilberforce, we can see Puritan radicalism reborn, shorn of its theological prejudices. Coleridge noted this rift in the tradition and took it as a blessing saying, 'It was God's mercy to our age that our Jacobins were infidels, and a scandel to sober Christians. Had they been like the old Puritans, they would have trodden Church and King to dust, at least for a time' (**71**, *Table Talk* ii, 68).

The point Coleridge makes is, I think, grossly overstressed. Militant atheism was rare even in the most 'Jacobin' of circles and in the British situation had no necessary association with practical anticlericalism which was indeed a major element in the whole ethos of Dissent. The 'Poor Labourer' who so naturally resented Archdeacon Paley's facile defence of the class system looked to 'the God of All Nature' to vindicate the cause of the oppressed people [**doc. 21**]. Tom Paine's powerful *Age of Reason*, however unorthodox, was not the work of an atheist. The Kilhamite 'New Connexion' were sometimes called 'Tom Paine Methodists' and chapels were described as Jacobin. Cobbett denounced everything—but not the idea of God. William Lovett was one of the many Chartists who came from a Methodist background and lived to see the preaching of 'Christian Chartism'. When in 1851 Charles Kingsley's sermon 'The Message of the Church to Labouring Men' was condemned by more orthodox clergy, a meeting of working men urged him to 'start a free church independent of episcopal authority'. Here is the reason for the continued acceptance of theism among those most opposed to the Established Church. Dissent, whether as to organisation or doctrine, always provided an alternative for those who found the Church of England uncongenial. Unitarianism drew off those who disliked traditional dissent. The Deists stood beyond the unitarians. Beyond them were the Chartist Churches; in a later generation Labour Churches and Ethical Churches were still endeavouring to maintain themselves in an even more rarified atmosphere. English people found no difficulty in the words later put into the mouth of a Thomas Hardy character that a man could be 'good but not religious good'. The Owenites evolved into Rational Religionists. It was well said— and ironically enough the words were once quoted by Wilberforce— that 'the form of the temple may continue when the *dii tutelares* have left it'. There was rarely any need for an Englishman to be forced to make a clean break with the religious pattern of life. It was rather a question of changing to a more congenial chapel.

Not till the 1850s—the end of the period under review—did the remnants of the Owenites, Painites, Chartists and others coalesce into a definitely Secularist Movement. Even then their basis was a rigidly ethical one and Christianity was condemned by a standard higher and more humane than that offered by the Bible which, rather than the Church, was the object of the early Secularist attacks (**45**). The idea of God was not easily banished from the early Victorian world picture, and many radicals found themselves forced or persuaded to come to terms with it. John F. Bray scathingly satirised the Christian faith in his *Voyage from Utopia* (**43**) but before the end of his life championed spiritualism and wrote in a theological jargon. (The Coming Age; God and Man a Unity). Richard Carlile, once the arch foe of God and King, lived to register as a Dissenting preacher and proclaim 'Christ is the only Radical Reformer'.

The threat of 'Jacobinism' (however loosely defined) to the Established Church was a very real one because of the association of the Church with the existing social order, [**doc. 6c**]. Whether

55

or not Jacobinism was in any sense a menace to the essential Christian faith is very doubtful indeed. Most respectable Latitudinarians were committed to little more than a 'cult of the Supreme Being'. To that extent they were at once with Robespierre himself. The validity of the Bible, the meaning of Christian doctrine, the relationship of faith and works, all these were being ardently debated by working men, but all concurred in seeing in the Evangelicals the defenders of a social order rather than the advocates of a disinterested morality and in Wilberforce a smiling hypocrite who not only bound the poor man with the chains of discriminatory laws but tried to make him grateful for them as well [**doc. 18a, d**].

9 The High Church Revival

The Church as well as the State was tried and refined in the crucible of the French Wars. Just as the trend towards parliamentary reform had been drowned in a flood of loud 'patriotism', not to reassert itself again until the postwar years, so too the Church took a harder line towards politically suspect dissent on the one hand and a friendlier one towards Catholicism as represented by the French Royalist refugees on the other. The great issue was clearly 'the Church versus liberalism', and political conformism the test of acceptable religious principles which could now be stretched to include a grateful and dependent Romanism. Among the Evangelicals, outward, religion was closely identified with the needs of the embattled state whilst 'inward' religion was broken down into the absolutely irreducible categories of one God *vis-à-vis* one soul. As an interim ethic in a world staggering under the final apocalyptic shocks—for so the Napoleonic Wars appeared to many—this was perhaps an acceptable view (so much is evidenced by the two movements of Brothers and Joanna Southcott) but in the postwar years new policies were necessary. In any case, by the 1830s, when the demand for new approaches reached its height, all the leading Evangelicals were dead. Granville Sharp and Venn had died in 1813, Thornton in 1815. Wilberforce died in 1833 and Simeon three years later. Shaftesbury, who died in 1885, was an isolated and almost embarrassing figure. It is curious and, as we shall see, not without significance that he was a cousin of Dr Pusey.

In the fifteen postwar years of Tory Rule (1815–30) we can see some superficial parallels to that last Tory heyday, the reign of Anne. The Church Building Society was actively backed by Parliament—ultimately to the extent of some £6 million—and through the 'National' Society (founded in 1811) the Church exercised a powerful influence over education. The continuing alliance of Church and State was happily symbolised by the Manners-Sutton clan, whose most notable achievement was to provide an Archbishop of

Canterbury whose son was Speaker of the House of Commons. Bishops (Van Mildert of Durham, for example) were preaching doctrines of apostolic succession and of priesthood that only escaped the name of Tractarian because that movement had not yet been invented. Then in 1821 that unrecognised storm warning the 'Peterborough Questions case' occurred. Dr Herbert Marsh, the Bishop of Peterborough, had refused to licence a new curate, John Green, because he, while willing enough to give the customary assent to the Thirty-nine Articles, would not accept the bishop's right to require him to tackle a supplementary list of eighty-seven theological questions and return 'short, plain, positive answers' on a printed form. The issue twice went up to the Lords before it was finally dropped. A popular commentator pointedly remarked that 'On neither occasion was a word uttered by any bishop but the one appealed against. Lord Carnarvon expressed his astonishment at their silence. . . . He declared that these spiritual peers, whose ample presence that night was certainly ornamental, though not apparently useful, were ready enough to give their opinion on constitutional questions, but had not a word to say on a matter peculiarly within their province. The truth was, they were unprepared' (**79**, i, bk. 2). The Bishop of Peterborough's attitude stands in sharp contrast to that implied by the normal usage of the eighteenth century on such occasions, an attitude summed up by Woodward (**7**) as follows: '[The Church] required conformity and left some doubt about the doctrine to which the faithful conformed.' Halévy (**4**) epitomises the case more brutally, saying: 'The material point was that nobody was obliged to believe the Thirty-nine Articles or even to read them', and in a footnote quotes Gisborn's *Duties of Man*, in which the question is discussed as one between the candidate and the legislature requiring the subscription. The bishop is hardly involved. One thinks, too, of James Woodforde's ordination examination (23 May 1763), which consisted of construing a passage from an epistle (**13**). The young gentleman thought he was hard done by: 'I was quite half an hour examining.' Plainly more rigorous standards were to be insisted upon for the new generation. (See **53** for other ordination anecdotes.)

The Church after the Napoleonic Wars was plainly more willing to assert itself as an estate of the realm, more conscious of its ancient spiritual authority and somewhat less willing to be the pliant tool of the politicians. Equally, its clergy had still to think out both the logical basis and the future implications of this new role. Coleridge, here as elsewhere a seminal thinker, wrote: 'My fixed Principle is; that a Christianity without a Church exercising spiritual authority is vanity and dissolution.' Soon a movement arose based on this very principle.

It is by no means to be wondered at that there was a demand for Church reform in the 1830s. The reform of Parliament itself in 1832 is rightly seen as a momentous measure in its implications if not in its actual details, but it is perhaps often misleadingly isolated from its proper context. The turn of the tide, the beginning of a phase in which British is distinguished from continental history by the fact that both the nation's major parties were favourable to some degree of reform, began in 1822 when the Liverpool cabinet was reorganised. The reform of Parliament by the Whigs was but the centrepiece of a varied display of reform gestures, each having its own justification. The major legislative reforms began in the religious field with the according of full civil rights to Protestant Dissenters (1828) and Roman Catholics (1829), then moved to the question of Parliament itself before going on to work through a list of varied social measures. We may specially note the Civil Marriages Act of 1836 as representing a further stage in the integrations of non-Anglicans into the general community.

The Radical demand for the exposure and reform of corruption as exemplified by *The Extraordinary Black Book* of 1831 were levelled as much at the Church as at the State and in the ranks of the Church itself there was recognition that some reform must come, preferably from within [**doc. 23**], if only to avoid more brutal surgery at the hands of unsympathetic outsiders, for there was a lively (and well-founded) fear of the Whigs as having no real attachment to Anglicanism as such but only as the faith currently subscribed to by the majority. In 1790 Fox had cogently argued; 'The truth of religion was not a subject for the discussion of Parliament; their duty only was to sanction that which was most universally approved'; and again: 'this opinion was sanctioned by the statutes which had passed, making one sort of religion the establishment of the north division of the kingdom and another sort of religion the establishment of the south (**52**) [**doc. 22**]. The views of Fox in the 1790s were those of the Whigs in general in the 1830s and these in turn had much in common with those of Warburton as expressed in his *Alliance of Church and State* of 1736, the sole distinction being that Warburton, as a bishop, believed the doctrines of the Church of England to be true independently of the fact of their being generally supported. The Whigs, in contrast, were regarded by godly men as being little better than atheists. Early in their term of office the Whigs had drafted reform proposals for the Church; commissioners were to take over the administration of Church assets, non-residence—and therefore plurality also—was to be done away with. The organisation and endowments of the sees were to be rationalised. When the Whig administration briefly yielded place to that of Sir Robert Peel the new government continued along the same lines and a report was issued. However, the Whigs were back in power again before the second report appeared and any positive action had been taken. This almost bipartisan treatment of the Church question illustrates the political view of the matter as a purely administrative one, a view acceded to by many leading Churchmen. (Blomfield's pious phrase in [**doc. 23**] does not really affect his line of argument.) The body of commissioners first set up included the two Archbishops as well as the Bishops of London, Lincoln and Gloucester. In 1840 all the bishops became *ex officio* members of the Ecclesiastical Commissioners. There was then much agreement on the policy of Church reform though a letter from Peel to the Bishop of London [**doc. 24**] reflects an odd reaction to the apparent ease with which the problem was being tackled.

The legislative achievements of the Whig reformers may be briefly recounted. The Ecclesiastical Commissioners were established as a permanent body. Clergy were at long last prevented from holding more than one living. New sees were created at Manchester and Ripon; parishes could now be divided; cathedral chapters were pruned of superfluous members and the released revenues diverted. All tithes were to be paid in money on a scale related to cereal prices, and finally the judicial committee of the Privy Council became the ultimate court of appeal in matters of Church discipline. The problem of church rates (for the purposes of maintaining the fabric of the parish church) had become acute in the postwar years but proved too difficult to bring to a final settlement before 1868. In England the necessary administrative reorganisation of the Church was carried through with much traditionalist protest but no real opposition. The consensus of informed opinion was with reform. The improvement in the tithe situation, for example, delivered a severe blow at rural anti-clericalism.

It was oddly enough in connection with proposed parallel reforms in the Church of Ireland where the abuses were so much more flagrant and the reforms so obviously more justifiable that the dispute was most bitter. In Ireland a nationwide system of parishes, clergy, cathedrals and bishops served the 'Church of Ireland' fraction of the nation. The Catholic majority, already ground down by the payment of rents to their absentee landlords, were also oppressed by the demand for tithe payments to this alien and (to them) heretical body. Popular feeling and popular action made the collection of tithes virtually impossible in many places. The clergy sought for their legal rights through the courts. One rector, Irvine Whitty, who did this overzealously, pressing forty-five tithe recovery claims in one session, was shot by his outraged involuntary parishioners. The people would not pay, the clergy could not live and, moreover, felt the rights of the legitimate church were at stake. State intervention and coercion led to popular violence. The Church of Ireland had plainly reached an impasse. The Whigs wished to go forward on the same rationalising lines as in England though the Irish situation meant that the results would be far more spectacular. In England a majority body needed administrative overhaul; in Ireland a minority institution created for proselytising purposes had manifestly failed in this end and now merely encumbered a resentful land.

The reforms proposed for Ireland involved scaling down the institutions and personnel of the Church to a level more appropriate to its real numerical support. Ultimately the logical step of dis-establishment was seen to be unavoidable but in the 'thirties abstract principle was invoked more frequently than logic. Those who hoped to salvage something from the wreck of Anglican hopes in Ireland reasonably thought that the surplus revenues of the remodelled church might be used for educational and philanthropic purposes. However, the idea of 'Appropriation' sparked off something like hysteria. Over ten years before, Brougham [**doc. 22**] had warned of the dangers of linking the English and Irish Church questions. This unwarranted confusion of two very different situations was the whole point and basis of the arguments of the new militant clericalism emerging at Oxford where John Keble, on 14 July 1833, devoted his Assize Sermon to the theme of 'National apostasy' and accused those in Parliament who wished to redistribute the surplus wealth of the beleaguered Church of Ireland of 'direct disavowal of the sovereignty of God'. 'I have ever considered and kept the day', wrote Newman, 'as the start of the religious movement of 1833' (**56**).

In a study of Anglicanism and popular religion, and even more so in a study terminating as this one does *c*. 1850, it is not necessary to devote a great deal of space to the Oxford or Tractarian Movement. However, in any study of the Anglican Church the movement cannot simply be passed over, it was too important, too vital. A brief description and some passing observations must therefore be included, if only for the sake of narrative continuity. In 1833 then, a group of young Oxford-based clerical academics took up arms in defence of the Church against the outrageous proposals of its would-be reformers. Theirs was a passionate reaffirmation of the autonomous nature of the Church and a call to its clergy to reassert their high calling as executive members of the only divinely founded society. After heroic literary efforts to expound these ideas and ideals to their fellow clergy, and monumental scholarly activity to vindicate Anglicanism as an authentic Church in no way inferior to the larger though no more legitimate Roman and Orthodox communions, Newman and some of his associates abandoned their cause and in 1845 crossed over to the Roman branch of the Church. In 1851 a second group followed them, chief among them being the future Cardinal Manning. So much then for the Movement's bare place in the chronology of the Church.

In his introduction to Newman's *Apologia pro vita sua*, Shane Leslie asked the question 'What was the Oxford Movement?' and answered thus: 'It was a religious revival which made the Church of England what it has been ever since, and restored the Roman Catholic body to the state of national consideration and respect it now enjoys. Both churches owe more to Newman than either can ever repay' (**56**). The motives that led to this revival are perhaps best sought for in the minds of its protagonists—and above all in that of Newman himself—rather than in any clash of classes or shifts in the economic foundations of power. It was an individual rather than a social movement. Families, Newman's own, for example, were deeply divided over the Oxford claims. Nevertheless, the movement can be related, albeit in negative fashion, to contemporary political trends. In a nutshell, their politics were grotesquely reactionary. As Newman himself put it, 'The vital question was, how were we to keep the Church from being liberalised?' (**56**). So reactionary (or so perceptive?) was Newman, that though he possessed a copy of Paine's *Rights of Man*, a bestseller among politically conscious working-men of his day, 'He kept it . . . under lock and key and let it out only to those who, he was assured, could come to no harm in consequence' (**9**). Nor was this tendency peculiar to Newman. In 1831 J. H. Froude, another 'Oxford Apostle', had written to Keble about rural discontent in Devonshire: 'Things are still in a bad way down here. The labouring population, as well as the farmers, seem thoroughly indifferent to the welfare of the parsons and squires. . . . I have now made up my sage mind that the country is too bad to deserve an Established Church' (**9**, p. 241). It is curious, too, to note the group's link with the Evangelicals. Newman again was typical of a trend. His family and background was Evangelical but with painful steps he trod the path to Rome. Spencer Perceval jnr. made a similar though even more exotic pilgrimage. Strange though it may seem there was logic of a sort in this spiritual emigration.

Perhaps the greatest *objective* achievement of Evangelicalism was its work as a spiritual police force in the days when the Jacobin was at the gate. It willingly subscribed to a political-religious relationship characteristic of the Hanoverian age. After the war the nakedness of the Evangelical cause was readily perceived. As a *religious* trend it lacked a social dimension [**doc. 18c**]. Now, moreover, in the eyes of the religiously hypersensitive, the godless were no longer across the Channel, they were entrenched in Whitehall (**52**) (**58**). The alliance of Church and State must be terminated and Erastian theories defied. Evangelicalism seemed to be played out. Shaftesbury was a lone survival into the Oxford generation. Tractarianism was in one sense a rediscovery of community in religion and a negation of the crude identifying of the community with the actual political State and Newman even wrote of 'the possibility of the Church's being made to dwell in the affection of the people at large', but there is no suggestion of democracy here. It was democracy that stamped Dissent with its hateful character.

If the tractarians were quite out of sympathy with the rising tide of political reform neither did they have any real contact with the religious traditions of the common people. On the subject of the medieval practice of fasting before communion Vaux remarks: 'The ancient reverential custom continued to be observed by religious people long before its revival by the so-called Tractarian movement'

(**21**). One might say the same about the practice of bowing to the altar (**9**, 32–3). Nevertheless the movement did have its genuine root in the English past. Newman's *via media* Anglicanism derived from the nonjurors and in a striking metaphor Shane Leslie (**56**) talks of Newman recovering their hidden seed from the cerements of the mummified Established Church and bringing it to flower and fruit. The nonjuring episcopate continued, tenuously, until 1805 into the lifetime or rather into the infancy of the men who made the Oxford Movement. A physical contact, a blessing even, might have been possible, though none took place. Newman's religion, despite his rhetorical arts, was a cerebral one and his own link with the nonjurors as with the primitive apostles was from book to book rather than from generation to generation.

After Newman left the English Church his movement regrouped its forces and marched on. By the 1850s its essential work—a new self-evaluation by the Church—had been achieved [**doc. 27**] and a new vision inspired it. Compare Newman's view in **doc. 25** with Warburton's matter of fact argument in [**doc. 1**]. Some of this reanimated High Church party devoted themselves to the byways of ritualism and its resultant litigation, others took their vision of the Church into the slums of the great cities and the still neglected rural areas. Their achievement in these fields was recognised even among their critics (for example, in the 1878 Presidential Address to the Evangelical 'Victoria Institute').

The deep concern of certain individuals over the state of the Church as it was in the 1830s was not confined to those who later emerged as the Tractarian movement. Two other 'shoots', the so called 'Irvingites' and the Plymouth Brethren, sprang from the same fertile soil, though they offered diametrically opposed solutions to the same basic questions. Neither of these became major popular movements though they were 'pointers' for trends of thought wider than themselves, iceberg tops of hidden masses of deeper disquiet. Their subsequent evolution, of the Brethren into a sect and of the Irvingites into nonentity vindicates the majority who chose still to cling to the National Church, which rode out this crisis as it has so many others.

As did the contemporary Oxford Movement, the sect later known as the Plymouth Brethren owed its emergence in the 1830s to the situation in Ireland. J. N. Darby (1800–82), a Church of Ireland curate in Wicklow, is attested as having been a veritable saint to the people of his parish and his ministry attracted many away from the Roman Church. This modest revival of Protestant hopes, for Darby was not alone in his successes, seems to have caused more concern than rejoicing in Archbishop Magee whose main worry seems to have been the political dependability of the newly converted. The Archbishop therefore insisted on new converts taking a political oath of allegiance and by thus identifying acceptance of the Reformed Faith with acquiescence in English political domination succeeded in thwarting all Darby's missionary endeavours. Conversions ceased, so Darby resigned in protest and began to associate with others who were aggrieved as he was and convinced that the State's control of the Church was the great scandal of the age. Darby, with Groves, Bellet, Cronin, Newton and others, by going back to the fountain head of Scripture, sought to revive simple Christian fellowship at grassroots level in place of the institutionalised and Erastian Church they had formerly served. The new fellowship prospered in England, particularly in the West Country, an association recalled by the movement's popular name. Having decided that authority over the Church did not rightfully belong to the State, the Brethren now began to differ among themselves about authority within their own body. Darby adopted an almost papal tone— indeed his followers were often simply known as Darbyites—and by 1845 we can discern the start of the rift between the 'Open' meetings and the avowedly sectarian 'Exclusive Brethren' led by Darby himself. The movement—simple, fundamentalist, sabbatarian, anticlerical—attracted much localised support, especially among the working people, and sometimes drew into itself entire congregations from outside as, for example, the Strict Baptists of Barnstaple, but this 'snowballing' was strictly limited and the hoped for leavening of the lump did not take place. Brethrenism now survives in the form of localised, almost hereditary communities who, as T.F.C. Stunt (**58**) has written 'almost rejoice in their diversity'.

The Irvingite or Catholic Apostolic Church offered yet a third response to the religious challenges of the day. Tractarians and Brethren had both looked back to the earlier Church for a firm and scriptural foundation on which to take their stand, the Tractarians to the developed Church of the Middle Ages and the Brethren to the almost pre-ecclesiastical days of the New Testament. The new movement accepted the thesis that the 1830s were indeed the latter days [**doc. 26**] and outbid rivals by confidently identifying themselves with the one true church now restored by God's direct intervention. It is a claim curiously parallel though in no way related to that of the contemporary Latter Day Saints of the U.S.A. The Irvingites gathered from diverse quarters to assume the roles of God's directly commissioned Latter Day Apostles. The new church had a double root, but it is logical to begin with Irving himself. Born in 1792 at Annan, Dumfries, Edward Irving went to Edinburgh University at the age of thirteen. After an academic career of great distinction he entered the Presbyterian ministry and was appointed as assistant to the well-known Thomas Chalmers in Glasgow. Irving became a brilliant preacher though in a baroque style and, as Chalmers observed, 'for connoisseurs only'. He gained a large personal following and in 1822 took over the Scotch Church in Hatton Garden, London. Here his ministry and notoriety reached its height. He preached the imminence of the Second Coming and (as even Arnold did) of the signs of the end of the age. On visits to Scotland he drew enormous audiences, on one occasion so large that the gallery of the church collapsed under the weight and several people were killed. It was this event that first brought Irving to national attention. His teachings seemed to find confirmation in an outbreak of 'signs' in 1830 among the Macdonald brothers' congregation at Port Glasgow and soon his own church in London was the scene of similar events. The gift of tongues appeared again and Irving's power was the fashionable topic of the day. In 1832 he was excommunicated by the Presbytery of London and barred from his ministry. In the year following he was ejected from the Church of Scotland entirely. Wealthy friends provided him with a chapel and began to evolve an elaborate cult known as the Holy Catholic Apostolic Church. Irving, however, played little active part in this. He had only another year to live and died, bewildered and broken, in 1834.

The men who gathered round Irving in his last years had for the most part Evangelical backgrounds. Notable among them was Henry Drummond, whose home at Albury was used by Irving as a place of study and meditation. Another such was Spencer Perceval jnr, son of the assassinated prime minister. Evangelicals had preached the end of the age for so long that it is not surprising to find them attracted to such a powerful preacher of the same message. Henry Bulteel came to the Irvingites from the Brethren and before that had been curate at St Ebbe's, Oxford. The group as a whole, like the earlier

Clapham Sect, was wealthy and influential, and in some cases at least the psychological push behind their support for the new cult was a pathological hatred and fear of democracy. F. C. Woodhouse inveighed against 'the wicked doctrine that all power is from the people' (**1**, vol ii p. 322) and it is symbolically apt that as the chief apostle of the restored church, J. B. Cardale, received his call, the Reform Bill was going through the House of Commons. It must have seemed that anarchy and divine order were racing neck and neck! Within six months of Irving's death, a quorum of twelve apostles had been assembled and were symbolically set apart for their work on 14 July 1835. Each congregation of 'the Catholic Apostolic Church now restored' had its own elaborate hierarchy from the presiding 'angel' through twenty-four priests to humbler deacons and doorkeepers. Tithes were exacted, but as this was not a church of the people finance was not a serious problem. An elaborate eclectic liturgy was published in 1842 typifying the movement's preoccupation 'with ritual, artistry and learning' (**1**). Irving himself played but little part in the new structure, being only 'angel' of his own congregation. He could hardly have been less. The end of the age did not come and the apostles clung together in the hostile world of Chartism, the 1848 revolutions and the Communist Manifesto. The horror of a second Reform Act had to be witnessed. One by one the apostles died and could not be replaced. The youngest of them just survived into the twentieth century and still the end had not come. The Apostles' splendid church in Gordon Square is now the Anglican chaplaincy for the students of London University. The main interest of this strange story is as a measure of the intensity of religious passions in the 1830s.

Part Three

ASSESSMENT AND AFTERMATH

Assessment and Aftermath

The year 1851 provides a natural termination for our period. As the year of the Great Exhibition it was an obvious time for moral as well as material stocktaking. It was also the year of the first—and only—census of church attendance (55). From the Anglican point of view the facts it revealed were daunting. Firstly, of some seven and a half million people who attended a place of worship on census day (30 March) less than four million had been to Anglican churches. In other words, something like half the nation's worshippers were Nonconformists. Secondly, in the great industrial cities there was simply not enough church accommodation for the inhabitants, had they desired to attend. In such places as Sheffield, Liverpool, Manchester and Birmingham seating was available for little more than one in three and in some cases for fewer than that. One hundred years of the alliance of Church and State, one hundred years of internal renewal and external remodelling, had not captured the masses for the Established Church. At the end of the eighteenth century the Church of England had theoretically provided seating accommodation for some 48 per cent of the population, though this figure is a national average concealing vast local differences.

The Church in 1851 could hardly look back on years of victory, though in fact it entered the next phase of its life in many ways better equipped than it had been in the 1750s. To begin with, overt unbelief was no longer rampant among the upper classes. It was one of the achievements of the Evangelical movement to have won over these, at least to the outward forms of faith. Family prayers and grace at meals, mourned by William Law as an extinct practice, were now usual in upper-class households. Secondly, the Church, after sustaining severe internal injuries was now on a firm yet adaptable footing on the basis of diversity in unity. An Anglo-Catholic party was balanced by an Evangelical or Low Church one, while the middle ground was held by a Broad Church (the term came into use in the 1850s) inheriting the old traditions of Latitudin-arianism and Comprehension. One was no longer either simply churchman or Nonconformist but varying types of 'churchmanship' had to be taken into consideration. This was a victory for both common sense and the original conception of the Church as *via media*. Thirdly, the years of political turmoil had been endured with-out the development of mass anticlericalism. The Church had retained the respect and affection of many ordinary people even outside its own ranks.

For students our period offers many still unresolved controversies and academic desiderata. For years the image of the Georgian Church was a somewhat tarnished one until Norman Sykes (**10**) began the long process of reappraisal. Here the question is one of our standard of judgment. It is quite obvious, for example, that the much admired Church of the seventeenth century displayed most of the same abuses as did the Georgians. Why then their differing reputations? But perhaps this is rather a question of historiography. A possibility for interesting local study would be that of Church–Dissenter relationships in specified communities. We know that Occasional Conformity was widely practised (**21**), and we know that many clergy were willing to build bridges across denominational barriers [**doc. 7b**]. We also know that the law's demand and social reality are often two quite different things. It would be of interest to pursue this theme in terms of family and local history. Another little explored field is that of the *effective* beliefs of the ordinary man as opposed to the creed he learned by heart but rarely understood. The vast but utterly disorganised archives of folklore contain much material on this topic. Work on it has hardly begun (**20**).

The greatest challenges of the period however, are those associated with Methodism. What was its character? A mere 'external irritation [**doc. 27**] or a movement by which 'England was for ever enriched' (**36**)? Can we subscribe to the picture of a soul-destroying reign of terror (**17**)? Once again the issue of effective as opposed to formal belief arises—the gulf between what the minister demanded and what the member actually did. Here again detailed local studies are demanded. Modern Methodists, too, have perhaps smoothed over the rougher features in their portraits of their ancestors. Rational and humane men (Oliver Goldsmith, for example) spoke of the early Methodists with sheer contempt. The language of the intem-perate Cobbett [**doc. 16**] is not unrepresentative here. And how well founded were the persistent stories of sexual licence at the love feasts [**doc. 12**]? It is odd that English sectarianism of this period should be, according to its own chroniclers at least, so apparently asexual. Most religious sects are prone to extend their theological criticisms to accepted property and marriage patterns. The English sects of our period seem to have had their eyes firmly fixed on the other world. Can this be true? Martin Madan, whose name still features in the Methodist hymn book, published a reasoned advocacy of polygamy. We must first, as E. P. Thompson has insisted, try to know what Methodism really was before we can discuss its impact and significance. There is no doubt, too, that the name Methodist was not only used very loosely but also concealed violent differences that flowed over into everyday life. An old Yorkshire lady of 'Primitive' background once said to me: 'It used to be a saying with us, "If you must cheat, cheat a Wesleyan".'

The classic question, however, is that raised by Hobsbawn (**31**). That John Wesley 'saved' England from revolution is still stated as a fact in popular evangelical literature and is found in most standard textbooks on Methodism (e.g. **36**, p. 265). We are still only scratching the surface of this question. Some of its complexities are suggested by Jackson [**doc. 15**]. Evangelicalism, too, poses its problems. What objective good did this movement do? What, if any, were its life enhancing qualities [**doc. 17**]? What were the deepest motives of its principals? Can we explain the paradox of Wilberforce, hated by the politically conscious working men of his day yet now acclaimed as one of the great humanitarians of his age? The undoubtedly sectarian movements (for Methodists would deny they should be categorised thus) are only now being recognised as being worthy of rational historical and social discussion(**17**). The outline stories of Joanna Southcott and Richard Brothers are accessible enough, but who were their supporters and how many of them were there? These people have been too readily dismissed as curiosities. They merit analysis as phenomena. Stark (**1**) tries to argue that all sects are based on 'out groups' excluded from the power structure but this is absurd when it is applied, for example, to Evangelicals. Nor is it very convincing to explain the movement of wealthy Irvingite aesthetes as a mere consequence of the humble Port Glasgow revival. The upheavals of the 1830s and the strange cross fertilisations of the Brethren, the Oxford Movement and the Irvingites have been fortunate enough to attract the attention of T. F. C. Stunt (**58**) who

73

in a series of minor papers and reviews has shown a stimulating approach to this period. We look forward to a major work from his pen.

Above and beyond all these questions for the student of history lies something of far wider significance. Can we discern any autonomous motivation (other than sheer vested interest) in the activity of the body we call the Church of England during this or indeed any other period? Do its activities proclaim it as a divine society or has it always been as Brougham suggests [**doc. 22**] a mere administrative convenience? Once the ecclesiastical arm of the Whig supremacy, it became 'the Tory Party at prayer'. Bishop Ken declared it to be 'holy, catholic and apostolic' but he became one of the nonjurors while the mainstream Church swore its fresh oath and soldiered on. The anguished Newman in another century pondered the same question and at last returned a long delayed answer. When Bishop Hoadley suggested that no existing body was to be identified as the actual Church of Christ, uproar resulted. Many it would seem could make the identification readily enough. Can we really see any essentially spiritual dimension in the lives of men like Blomfield (**53**) or Warburton? Many historians must have been, many must indeed still be, actual or nominal Christians. None, since Bede, has to my knowledge made the life of the Church the core or basis of their historical analysis of a period. Is the history of the Church a theme in itself or merely part of an ideological superstructure? This is the major question.

We have briefly touched on some of the problems posed for the student by the events of the period 1750 to 1850. What was the significance of the period as a whole for the generations coming after? It was an age that saw the development of two challenges to every established order—the industrial revolution in Britain and the political revolution in France. It was an age when, for the first time, viable alternatives to the prevailing mode of life were seen to exist. The Church rose to neither challenge. It neither discerned the enormity of the industrial revolution which was henceforward to condition the whole of man's life, nor did it see any justification for the claims of the masses to some larger place in the political structure. The efforts of the Church were most obviously confined to the defence of things as they were. The Church was not devoid of answers to the challenges of the times, but all split on the same rock. Methodism aimed at a non-competitive revivalism of socially conservative character. It became an alternative to the Church and by the 1850s an increasingly liberal one. The Evangelicals were willing enough to face up to social abuses (slavery, child labour and so on) in isolation, but bent their main efforts to defending the social order in which these abuses flourished. The Tractarians, too, were at first merely reactionary. As the nineteenth century drew to a close the Church was coming to grips with the realities around it (**12**), but the high tide of opportunity had passed. Secularism was an established force in the working class world. Christianity was no longer the major source of practicable (and admirable) social morality (**45**). Nor, even among those who remained within the theistic fold, was the Church the unchallenged pastor. It was the 'nonconformist conscience' that took most readily to the 'social gospel' and became a power in the land.

The period we have reviewed must, I fear, wear some drab discouraging label—'the Age of Lost Opportunities' perhaps or 'The Unimaginative Age'. As the nineteenth century ran on, religion was in active development over the widest spectrum and to the furthest horizons. Unitarianism, Spiritualism and Theosophy flourished. The Roman Church revived and may yet become the residuary legatee of all the religion of the Western World. Buddhism and Hinduism have attracted the attention of both Europe and America. 'Jehovah's Witnesses' have increased phenomenally. Christian Science and the Church of Latter Day Saints are now well-established middle-class cults. Eastern Orthodoxy is attracting more and more attention. It is beyond our wildest imaginings that any substantial body of people will ever again say with Fielding's Mr Thwackum: 'When I mean religions, I mean the Christian religion; and not only the Christian religion, but the Protestant religion; and not only the Protestant religion, but the Church of England.'

Part Four

DOCUMENTS

Bishop Warburton's defence of the idea of an Established Church

This extract, as much by its assumptions as by its positive arguments, is very representative of eighteenth-century 'Establishment' thinking. Warburton (1698–1779), a scholar and literary commentator rather than theologian, is also in his whole career typical of this phase of Church history. The source of this document is his famous 'Alliance between Church and State', originally published in 1736 but reissued with amendments in 1748 and 1766. Its subtitle is 'The Necessity and Equity of an Established Religion and a Test Law demonstrated'. Like all eighteenth-century philosophers, the Bishop claimed to look at his subject objectively and dispassionately. Although his book has been considered as the lowest possible view of the Church–State relationship, Warburton denied he was an Erastian. He saw parallel and allied civil and religious structures as reflecting the Body–Soul relationship as existing in the individual. He saw Church and State as 'two parties in the same cause, engaged in the same encounter'. His chosen key word was 'Alliance'. This, however, suggests some equality—of nominal status if not of actual power—between the allied parties, and equality with the State structure was rarely claimed for the Church at this period. It is a strangely medieval conception. In practice the Hanoverian Age made so little distinction between Church and State that the concept of Alliance must have seemed quite superfluous.

1. Opinions concerning the nature of the Deity so entirely influence all religious practice that *this* invariably takes its character from *those* and becomes more or less perfect as those are nearer to or further from the truth. On which account the greatest care is to be taken to preserve opinions pure and untainted. But this cannot be done but by a SOCIETY as we may understand from the very mention of those two ways which all societies have ever put into practice. 1. By reducing men's beliefs to one common formulary. And 2. By making the profession of that formulary the term of communion. For by this means there is a summary of belief in aid of the ignorant, and a common repository that men may always have recourse to for information . . . it is to be observed that the wider the bottom is made, and the more general the terms of communion

(consistent with the being of a society) the wiser and juster is that religious institution.

2. The several acts of religious worship are correspondent to the sentiments arising in us from our meditations on the several relations we stand in towards God and instituted with design to aid and improve those sentiments. Now, as meditations not tempered with these outward acts, are apt . . . to fly out into enthusiasm, so outward acts not regulated by nor adapted to these meditations are as subject to degenerate into a childish unmeaning superstition. And, how much enthusiasm depraves all the faculties of the mind, how much superstition dishonours the service of our Maker, is disputed by no one acquainted with the nature and effects of these direful evils. The greatest care, therefore, is to be taken that the solemn acts of religion be preserved, simple, decent and significative. But then this can only be done by providing persons set apart for this office; whose peculiar employment it shall be to preside in, direct and superintend the ritual of worship, lest anything childish, profane or superstitious should (as it certainly would if left to everyone's fancy) obtrude itself into religious service. Now public officers and ministers must act by some common policy, which may regulate and settle their several employments, powers and subordinates. But that policy is no other than the laws of a society, properly so called. What hath been said here is sufficient to manifest the Divine Wisdom of the Author and Finisher of our Faith who, revealing the will of His heavenly Father to mankind, actually formed our holy religion into a society, on a common policy, with public rites, proper officers and a subordination of the ministry . . . which justifies an establishment wherever the religion professed is the Christian.

William Warburton, *Alliance between Church and State*, in *Works*, 1811, vii, 59–60.

'The great man of a parish'

This document excellently illustrates the integration of Church and 'State' at parish level. It provides the practical refutation of any theory of 'alliance'.

It is a difficult matter to decide, which is looked upon as the greatest man in a country church, the parson or his clerk. The latter is most certainly held in higher veneration, where the former happens to be only a poor curate, who rides post every Sabbath from village to village, and mounts and dismounts at the church door. The clerk's office is not only to tag the prayers with an Amen, or usher in the sermon with a stave; but he is also the universal father to give away the brides, and the standing godfather to all the newborn bantlings. But in many places there is a still greater man belonging to the church than either the parson or the clerk himself. The person I mean is the Squire; who, like the King, may be styled Head of the Church in his own parish. If the benefice be in his own gift, the vicar is his creature, and of consequence, entirely at his devotion; or, if the care of the church be left to a curate, the Sunday fees of roast beef and plum pudding, and a liberty to shoot in the manor, will bring him as much under the Squire's command as his dogs and horses. For this reason the bell is often kept tolling and the people waiting in the churchyard an hour longer than the usual time; nor must the service begin until the Squire has strutted up the aisle, and seated himself in the great pew in the chancel. The length of the sermon is also measured by the will of the Squire, as formerly by the hour glass: and I know one parish where the preacher has always the complaisance to conclude his discourse, however abuptly, the minute the Squire gives the signal, by rising up after his nap.

William Cowper (1731–1800), from a letter to Lady Hesketh in *Selected English Essays* ed. W. Peacock (World's Classics).

The character of a clergyman

It is interesting to compare this description with that of the saintly parson of Goldsmith's 'Deserted Village'. There is little doubt as to which description is more typical. Law gave up his fellowship at Cambridge rather than take the oath to George I, but he did not become prominent among the Nonjurors.

Cognatus is a sober, regular clergyman, of good repute in the world, and well esteemed in his parish. All his parishioners say he is an honest man, and very notable at making a bargain. The farmers listen to him with great attention, when he talks of the properest time of selling corn.

He had been for twenty years a diligent observer of markets, and has raised a considerable fortune by good management.

Cognatus is very orthodox, and full of esteem for our English Liturgy; and if he has not prayers on Wednesdays and Fridays, it is because his predecessor had not used the parish to any such custom.

As he cannot serve both his livings himself, so he makes it a matter of conscience to keep a sober curate upon one of them, whom he hires to take care of all the souls in the parish at as cheap a rate as a sober man can be procured.

Cognatus has been very prosperous all his time; but still he has had the uneasiness and vexations that they have, who are deep in worldly business. Taxes, losses, crosses, bad mortgages, bad tenants, and the hardness of the times, are frequent subjects of his conversation; and a good or a bad season has a great effect upon his spirits.

Cognatus has no other aim in growing rich, but that he may leave a considerable fortune to a niece, whom he has politely educated in expensive finery, by what he has saved out of the tythes of two livings.

The neighbours look upon Cognatus as a happy clergyman, because they see him (as they call it) in good circumstances, and some of them intend to dedicate their own sons to the church, because they see how well it has succeeded with Cognatus, whose father was but an ordinary man.

William Law, *A Serious Call to a Devout and Holy Life*, 1729, xiii.

A country parish

Although Goathland was thinly populated, remote and underendowed, the situation portrayed in this document was not untypical. In many such areas dissent was virtually unknown. The last sentence of item 8 reminds us that the Wesleyan and Evangelical fervour was originally that of clergyman and not of hungry flocks demanding more spiritual nourishment. The same was the case with the Oxford Movement.

1. We have in the Chappellry of Goathland FourtyFour Families Of which number one is Popish which is the only Dissenting Family we have in this place.
2. We have no Meeting House either Licensed or unlicensed in our Chappellry.
3. There is sometimes here a privi or petty school taught by a Weaver, but no endowed one. He carefully instructs the children commited to him in the principles of the Christian Religion according to the Doctrine of the Church of England. . . .
4. We have no Alms House, Hospital or any other Charitable Endowment, neither has anything been left for the repair of our chapel or any other pious use.
5. . . . The Salary being poor is not sufficient to maintain a Residing Curate.
7. I do not know of any such who are unbaptiz'd come to Church nor Any, who are of competent age not Confirm'd.
8. Public Service is performed here once every Three weeks in the afternoon, and Four times a year in the forenoon on Sundays. The yearly salary accrueing the Minister which is raised by way of Assessment being only Four Pounds. The inhabitants are well satisfied with the Service.
9. I Chatechise in this Chappl Four times in the year and in Lent every Sunday when I am there. . . .
10. The Sacrament of the Lord's Supper is administered Twice in the Year viz. Easter and Christmas. We have generally betwixt seventy and eighty Communicants And Easter last we had Eighty-six.

11. . . . I have not had lately any reason to refuse the Sacrament to any of them.

Archbishop Herring's Visitation Report on the Chappellry of Goathland, York Diocese 1743. (Jonathan Robinson visiting curate)

A curate solicits a gift from a wealthy lady

The use of literary material as documentation must always be a little suspect, but such a passage as this makes many valuable points, amply reinforced by other more direct evidence. The interest of the Church is aroused only after *the Baptists have 'got possession'. In much the same way the 'National' School Society of 1811 was supported to oppose the Dissenting/Secularist 'British' schools. The curate sees himself as going to Ecclefigg to civilise 'a parcel of brutes'. It is all too true to life.*

'I came here this morning with a view to beg of you . . . a subscription to a school. I and Dr Boultby intend to erect one in the hamlet of Ecclefigg, which is under our vicarage of Whinbury. The Baptists have got possession of it. They have a chapel there, and we want to dispute the ground.'

'But I have nothing to do with Ecclefigg. I possess no property there.'

'What does that signify? You're a churchwoman, ain't you?'

' . . . I am a churchwoman, certainly.'

'Then you can't refuse to contribute in this case. The population of Ecclefigg are a parcel of brutes; we want to civilise them.'

'Who is to be the missionary?'

'Myself, probably.'

'You won't fail through lack of sympathy with your flock.'

'I hope not—I expect success; but we must have money. There is the paper. Pray give a handsome sum.'

Charlotte Bronte, *Shirley*, 1849; ch. 15

A rector explains a distasteful situation

Rector Wilmot who wrote these notes seems unwilling to admit the possibility of reasoned disagreement with the Establishment. The new Baptists seek to be 'of consequence', they are 'worthless' and 'hypocrites'. The parents of the unbaptised do not understand what they have read. The seceders leave the Church because they dislike the government. All these things, however, may be read another way.

[**a**] I am sorry to say that in the township of Smalley the Dissenters have gained ground considerably. The General Baptists as they call themselves have erected a handsome building for their meeting and by making many of the principal farmers trustees for the building they have created in their minds an idea of consequence which they are proud of possessing, and are led to consider it their interest to promote separation from the Church. One circumstance however I cannot help noting of these pretenders to more than ordinary sanctity— that with the exception of a few of them, they have always been considered by me as the most worthless characters in my Parish. And as I have never witnessed a change in their conduct to have been attendant on their religious profession I own I cannot divest myself of the opinion that their schism has more hypocrisy than religious zeal for its basis. (Morley 1800)

[**b**] I am inclined to believe that about one third of the children born are not baptised. For this circumstance I believe we are indebted to the works of the infamous Paine which have eradicated the principles of religion from the minds of the lower orders of the people; who not having leisure to study what they read are caught by the sound of words, and not by their reasoning. (Smalley 1798?)

[**c**] I do not however think that a total indifference to Religion increases. Tis more from disaffection to the Established Government that induces the lower order of the people to separate themselves from the church which they consider as part of that

Government than from any real difference of opinion on the effect of religion.

Extracts from comments in the Parish Registers of Morley and Smalley, Derbyshire, 1777 to 1801. MS copy in Derby Borough Library. These quotations taken from *Local Population Studies Magazine and Newsletter*, no. 2, Spring 1969.

document 7 a, b, c
An Anglican looks at the Dissenters

Daniel Defoe's 'The Shortest Way with Dissenters' although written in the reign of Anne is a brilliant documentation of certain aspects of the Anglican–Dissenter relationship throughout our period. George Saintsbury has written: '. . . the reader may amuse himself if he likes by meditating whether the "Shortest Way" is irony or not. My own opinion is that it is not; being a simple statement of the views of the other side.'

[a] You have butchered one king, deposed another king, and made a mock king of a third, and yet you could have the face to expect to be employed and trusted by the fourth. Anybody that did not know the temper of your party would stand amazed at the impudence, as well as folly, to think of it.

Your management of your Dutch monarch, whom you reduced to a mere King of Clouts, is enough to give any future princes such an idea of your principles as to warn them sufficiently from coming into your clutches; and God be thanked the Queen is out of your hands, knows you, and will have a care of you.

Then, in a more conciliatory tone, we get:
[b] Let us examine for what it is that this nation is divided into parties and factions, and let us see how they can justify a separation, or we of the Church of England can justify our bearing the insults and inconveniences of the party.

One of their leading pastors, and a man of as much learning as most among them, in his answer to a pamphlet, entitled 'An Inquiry into the Occasional Conformity', has these words, p. 27: 'Do the religion of the Church and the meetinghouses make two religions? Wherein do they differ? The substance of the same religion is common to them both; and the modes and accidents are the things in which only they differ.' P. 28: 'Thirty-nine articles are given us for the summary of our religion; thirty-six contain the substance of it, wherein we agree; three the additional appendices about which we have some differences.'

And finally, a return to the 'hard line':
[c] The humour of the Dissenters has so increased among the people that they hold the church in defiance, and the House of God is an abomination among them; nay, they have brought up their posterity in such prepossessed aversions to our holy religion that the ignorant mob think we are all idolators and worshippers of Baal, and account it a sin to come within the walls of our churches.

The primitive Christians were not more shy of a heathen temple or of meat offered to idols, nor the Jews of swine's flesh, than some of our Dissenters are of the Church, and the divine service solemnised therein.

J. Saintsbury, ed, *Political Pamphlets*, 1892, pp. 27, 42, 45.

document 8 a, b
The intolerance of the Church: an embittered view

Although Loveless was not perhaps such a political innocent as in his pamphlet he claims to have been, his words are still a powerful indictment of those clergymen who were only too ready to offer 'upbraiding and taunting' to men caught in the trap of the law. Note, too, that by 1834 a Wesleyan accepts the title of Dissenter without comment.

[a] *Feb. 1834, Loveless is in prison at Dorchester, waiting for the Assizes.*

In this situation the chaplain of the prison paid us a visit, to pour a volley of instruction into our ears; but, as it was mixed up in the cup of abuse, it did not exactly relish with me. After upbraiding and taunting us with being discontented and idle, and wishing to ruin our masters, he proceeded to tell us that we were better off than our masters. . . . He inquired if I could point out anything more that might be done to increase the comfort of the labourer. I told him I thought I could. . . . I thought gentlemen wearing the clerical livery, like himself, might do with a little less salary. . . .

'Is that how you mean to do it?' said he. 'That is one way I have been thinking of, Sir.'

[**b**] I am from principle, a Dissenter, and by some, in Tolpuddle, it is considered as the sin of witchcraft; nay, there is no forgiveness for it in this world nor that which is to come* . . . and many a curious tale might be told of men who were persecuted, banished and not allowed to have employ if they entered the Wesleyan Chapel at Tolpuddle.

George Loveless of Tolpuddle, 'The Victims of Whiggery' 1837, pp. 7, 11.

document 9 a, b
A liberal clergyman mocks the opponents of Catholic Emancipation

In his defence of Catholic integrity, Sydney Smith also manages to strike a blow at those clergymen who put tithe paying in the forefront of Christian practice. Note also the description of Catholics as 'dissenters' as in strict law they were.

* Compare Newman in a sermon of 1829, 'There is not a Dissenter living but, inasmuch, and so far as he dissents, is in a sin' (**9**), chap. 7, ii.

[**a**] The Catholic not respect an oath! Why not? What upon earth has kept him out of Parliament, or excluded him from all the offices whence he is excluded, but his respect for oaths? There is no law which prohibits a Catholic to sit in Parliament. There could be no such law; because it is impossible to find out what passes in the interior of any man's mind. Suppose it were in contemplation to exclude all men from certain offices who contended for the legality of taking tithes: the only mode of discovering *that fervid love of decimation which I know you to possess* would be to tender an oath 'against that damnable doctrine, that it is lawful for a spiritual man to take, abstract, appropriate, subduct or lead away the tenth calf, sheep, lamb ox, pigeon, duck,' etc., etc., etc., and every other animal that ever existed, of which of course the lawyers would take care to enumerate. Now this oath I am sure you would rather die than take; and so the Catholic is excluded from Parliament because he will not swear that he disbelieves *the leading doctrines of his religion*! The Catholic asks you to abolish some oaths which oppress him; your answer is that he does not respect oaths. Why then subject him to the test of oaths? The oaths keep him out of Parliament; why, then, he respects them. Turn which way you will, either your laws are nugatory, or the Catholic is bound by religious obligations as you are; but no eel in the wellsanded fist of a cook-maid, on the eve of being skinned, ever twisted and writhed as an orthodox parson does when he is compelled by the gripe of reason to admit anything in favour of a dissenter.

[**b**] What are your dangers which threaten the Establishment? —Reduce this declamation to a point and let us understand what you mean. The most ample allowance does not calculate that there would be more than twenty members who were Roman Catholics in one house, and ten in the other, if the Catholic emancipation were carried into effect. Do you mean that these thirty members would bring in a bill to take away the tithes from the Protestant, and to pay them to the Catholic clergy? . . . Do you fear for your tithes, or your doctrines, or your person, of the English Constitution? Every fear, taken separately, is so glaringly absurd, that no man has the folly or the boldness to state it. Every one conceals his ignorance, or his

baseness, in a stupid general panic, which, when called on, he is utterly incapable of explaining.

Sydney Smith, Letter ii of *Peter Plymley's Letters* (1807), in *Political Pamphlets* ed. G. Saintsbury, 1892.

document 10 a–d

Some unauthorised uses of Bible and Prayer Book

These samples of well established popular custom are evidences of a world of thought and action which we still know too little. One must never forget that a Bible could be used for a variety of purposes. It would be arbitrary to select only those uses approved by the clergy as evidence of the nature of popular religion.

[a] One Susannah Haynokes, an elderly woman, of Wingrove, near Aylesbury, Bucks, was accused by a neighbour for bewitching her spinning wheel, so that she could not make it to go round, and offered to make oath of it before the magistrate; on which the husband, in order to justify his wife, insisted on her being tried by the church Bible, and that the accuser should be present. Accordingly she was conducted to the parish church, where she was stripped of all her clothes, to her shift and under-coat, and weighed against the Bible; when, to the no small mortification of the accuser, she outweighed it and was honourably acquitted of the charge.

The Gentleman's Magazine, 1759.

[b] Opening the Bible on this day is a superstitious practice still in common use in some parts of the country, and much credit is attached to it. It is usually set about with some little solemnity in the morning before breakfast, as the ceremony must be performed fasting. The Bible is laid on the table unopened, and the parties who wish to consult it are then to open it in succession. They are not at liberty to choose any particular part of the book, but must open it at random. Wherever this may happen to be, the enquirer is to place his

finger on the chapter, contained in the two open pages, but without any previous perusal or examination. The chapter is then read aloud and commented on by the people assembled. It is believed that the good or ill fortune, the happiness or misery of the consulting party, during the ensuing year, will be in some way or other described and foreshown by the contents of the chapter.

J. Brand's *Observations on Popular Antiquities*, rev. edn, 1848, vol. i, on New Year's Day.

[c] When you go to bed, place under your pillow a common prayer book, open at the part of the matrimonial service in which is printed, 'With this ring I thee wed'. Place on it a key, a ring, a flower, a sprig of willow, a small heart-cake, a crust of bread and the following cards, viz. the ten of clubs, nine of hearts, ace of spades and the ace of diamonds; wrap all these round in a handkerchief of thin gauze or muslin. On going into bed cross your hands and say—

> 'Luna, every woman's friend,
> To me thy goodness condescend;
> Let me this night in visions see
> Emblems of my destiny,'

ibid., ii, 33.

This charm used at the time of the Harvest Moon was to induce pre-dictive dreams. It ultimately derives from an earlier chapbook, 'Mother Bunch's Closet Newly Broke Open'.

[d] It is customary in Yorkshire, for the common people to sit and watch in the church porch on St Mark's Eve, April 25th, from eleven o'clock at night till one in the morning. The third year (for this must be done thrice) they are supposed to see the ghosts of all those who are to die the next year, pass by into the church, which they are said to do in their usual dress, and precisely in the order of time in which they are doomed to depart. . . . Those who are to die remain in the church, but those who are to recover return, after a longer or shorter time,

in proportion to the continuance of their future sickness. When any one sickens who is thought to have been seen in this manner, it is presently whispered about that he will not recover, for that such or such a one, who has watched St. Mark's Eve, says so. The superstition is in such force that, if the patients themselves hear of it, they almost despair of recovery.

ibid., St Mark's Day. pp. 192–3.

Samuel Bamford in his 'Early Days' (1848) recounts the gruesome story of Old Johnny Johnson the sexton of Middleton (Lancs) who kept watch in this way—and saw a figure he recognised as his own! 'He had then seen enough, and with all speed he hastened to his home, became very thoughtful, soon after sickened and within the twelve months he died.' The story was told of other sextons in other places, too.

Popular anticlericalism

Folklore and custom are as yet only ill exploited as sources of social 'documentation'. One reason for this is shifting and evanescent nature of the material. Folk art on the other hand is much more easily handled. 'Staffordshire' figures, for example, may be dated with reasonable accuracy and their mass market proves the congeniality to the people of the sentiments they portrayed—or implied.

> Hob's wife and sow—as gossips tell
> Both at a time in pieces fell.*
> The Parson comes, the pig he claims
> And the good wife with taunts inflames
> But she, quite arch bowed low and smiled
> Kept back the pig and held the child.
> The priest looked gruff, the wife look'd big
> Z. . . . .ds, Sir; quoth she, no child, no pig!

(Verse inscribed on Liverpool mug of second half of 18th century. Victoria and Albert Museum 93–1879).

* Euphemism for giving birth.

There are many terser references to the same theme. One type of Toby jug, for example, bears the inscription, 'I will have no child but the X pig'. *Mugs sometimes have on them verses beginning with the words,* 'In Country Village lives a Vicar/Fond as they all are of Tithes and Liquor'. *Ralph Wood of Burslem made (c. 1770?) a figure group entitled* 'The Vicar and Moses', *in which the clergyman sleeps in the pulpit while the clerk below conducts the service. A 'sequel piece' made by Enoch Wood (d. 1840) is* 'The Parson and Clerk' *in which the drunken vicar is seen safely home by the faithful Moses. (In contrast to this tradition, there is also much reference to Dissenters as drinking excessively. One thinks of 'the Shepherd' in Pickwick. In Charlotte Brontë's 'Shirley', three Dissenters are depicted; Moses Barraclough the Ranter, Michael Hartley, 'that mad Calvinist and Jacobin' and 'the fat Dissenter . . . a spirit merchant by trade' routed in the clash of the Sunday Schools. All three are shown as too fond of the bottle.)*

Dr K. M. Briggs has called my attention to another reported 'tenth child' custom that reflects a more genial relationship between parson and parishioner. If a tenth child was born while the rest were still alive it was presented for christening with a sprig of myrtle in its cap. The vicar was bound by custom to pay for its schooling. (C. M. Yonge, An Old Woman's Outlook on a Hampshire Village, 1896, p. 200.) This appears to be the sole reference to the custom.

document 12 a, b

Love feasts

[a] *In some notes 'On worship' Hugh Bourne, the Primitive Methodist gave these instructions for the conduct of love feasts.*

Love feasts usually open with singing and prayer. A piece is then sung by way of asking a blessing; after which the bread and water are served out, the Love feast collection is made, and a piece sung by way of returning thanks. The preacher makes a few remarks; the people rise in succession, and speak their own experience; and distant comers sometimes say a little about the works of God in other places. But none are allowed to run into useless exhortations, drag out to tedious lengths, or to speak unprofitably of others; and above all not to reflect upon or find fault, either with individuals or societies. And it is the preacher's painful duty to stop all who attempt to trespass. He has to preserve the Love feast in its clear and pure course, in order that the people may grow into faith, and that the Holy Ghost may descend.

Singing and prayer are occasionally introduced; and the Love feast finally closes with prayer.

Bourne's Large Hymn Book, 1829.

[**b**] *De Brantôme (c. 1530–1614) reports substantially the same story of the Huguenot congregation in the Rue St Jacques (Paris) in the time of Henry II, vividly illustrating the stability over the centuries of these hostile rumours about 'heretics'.*

When the minister finished his sermon he ended by recommending charity, and immediately after that all the candles were put out and, there and then, pairing off, men and women, Christian brother and sister showed each other charity, sharing it all out one with another according to their whim and ability. I cannot really affirm that all of this was so, but I was certainly assured that it was, though it is quite possible that it is all pure falsehood and deception.

De Brantôme (**66**), Essay I.

documents 13 a, b
Myths of Methodism

All through his long life John Wesley expounded opinions on a great variety of subjects. Exclusion is the difficulty. I have therefore concentrated on two points only, both aspects of what might be called the myths of Methodism: namely that it drew its members from the 'outcast' classes and that its existence as a movement presented no objective challenge to the Established order of the Church.

[a] To 'John Smith', i.e. Thomas Secker, Bishop of Oxford, later Archbishop of Canterbury(??), 25 June 1746.

What is the end of all ecclesiastical order? Is it not to bring souls from the power of Satan to God, and to build them up in His fear and love? Order, then, is so far valuable as it answers these ends; and if it answers them not it is nothing worth. Now, I would fain know, where has order answered these ends? Not in any place where I have been;— not among the tinners in Cornwall, the keelmen at Newcastle, the colliers in Kingswood or Staffordshire; not among the drunkards, swearers, Sabbath-breakers of Moorfields, or the harlots of Drury Lane. They could not be built up in the fear and love of God while they were open barefaced servants of the devil; and such they continued, notwithstanding the most orderly preaching both in St Luke's and St Giles's Church. One reason whereof was, they never came near the church, nor had any desire or design so to do, till, by what you term 'breach of order', they were brought to fear God, to love Him and keep His commandments.

[b] To Dr Pretyman Tomline, Bishop of Lincoln, 1790.

The Methodists in general, my Lord, are members of the Church of England. They hold all her doctrines, attend her service, and partake of her sacraments. They do not willingly do harm, but do what good they can to all. To encourage each other herein, they frequently spend an hour together in prayer and mutual exhortation. Permit me to ask, *Cui bono*, 'For what reasonable end,' would your Lordship drive these people out of the Church? Are they not as quiet, as inoffensive nay as pious, as any of their neighbours? except perhaps here and there an hair brained man who knows not what he is about. Do you ask 'Who drives them out of the Church?' Your Lordship does; and that in the most cruel manner—yea and the most disingenuous manner. They desire a licence to worship God after their own conscience. Your Lordship refuses them it, and then punishes them for not having a licence! So your Lordship leaves them only this alternative, 'Leave the Church or starve.' And is it a Christian, yea a Protestant bishop that so persecutes his own flock?

John Wesley, *Selected Letters of John Wesley*, (**37**).

Methodist conversions

At about this time (i.e. 1786) or a little before, there began to
preach among the Methodists of Easingwold one who was led
to do so by a remarkable providence. John Crosby . . . was
living as a farm servant with Mrs Stillingfleet, and on one
Sabbath morning after returning from church Mrs S. said to
him, 'John, you must explain the Lord's Prayer in the family
tonight.' . . . he retired to his room, got his Bible, meditated on
the selected portion and earnestly implored the Divine assistance. When the time came he, in much fear, made the attempt
and God followed it with extraordinary marks of approbation.
Mrs S. found peace with God whilst he was speaking. A son and
daughter and the servant maid were convinced of sin. . . .
Several days after this interesting evening, the little girl who
had experienced the pardon of her sins was found burning her
playthings. Her mother told her not to burn them, for though
she would use them no more, yet they might be sold and so be
the means of doing some good; to which the child made this
striking answer, 'So Saul thought, when he spared the best of
the sheep and oxen to sacrifice to God; but you know, Mother,
Samuel condemned him for not having destroyed them all.

Early Methodism (**30**), pp. 9, 10.

Two faces of a Wesleyan minister

*Robert Newton (1780–1864), to whom these extracts refer, was a
representative figure of 'respectable' Methodism. His 'Life' by Thomas
Jackson, 1855, is an invaluable source of fact and anecdote. Newton
was a close associate of Jabez Bunting.*

[**a**] Before he left the Holmfirth Circuit [*in 1812*] he was subjected to painful trials arising from the agitated state of society
in his neighbourhood. An imaginary personage, bearing the

name of General Ludd, was said to be arranging his plans for the cure of existing evils, and to avenge the cause of the poor . . . marauding parties sallied forth during the night, breaking machinery in factories, stealing fire arms in private houses, and plundering defenceless families. The fire-arms that were thus collected . . . could not be discovered. It was at length suspected that the roof of a chapel in Mr Newton's Circuit was occupied as a depot for this kind of stolen property. It was accordingly searched, but no fire-arms were found; yet the answers of the chapelkeeper, when questioned on the subject, were so equivocal and unsatisfactory, as to produce an impression that, with his connivance, the place had been so occupied. He was therefore dismissed from his situation.

[b] During his superintendency of the Liverpool South Circuit [1826–9], an incident occurred which places his uprightness and fidelity in a striking light. A love-feast was appointed to be held in the Pitt-Street chapel, and a comparatively poor man was one of the doorkeepers, whose duty it was to inspect the Society-tickets of the people as they entered. A wealthy member of the Society, forgetting at the time the respect that is due to rule, to office and even to human nature, attempted to enter into the chapel without presenting his certificate of membership; and, on being expostulated with, rudely pushed the doorkeeper aside, and otherwise treated him with contumely. The matter was complained of in the Leaders' Meeting and the Class-Leader of the offender apologised for the outrage, stating that the man was sorry for what he had done. Mr Newton observed that this was not sufficient; the offence was public; it was an open contempt of rule and order; and an apology merely sent through a third party, and not even offered to the man who had been personally aggrieved and resisted in the discharge of his duty, could not be accepted. Wealth should rather be regarded as an incentive to civility, than as a justification of rudeness. The offender attended the next meeting of the Leaders, confessed that he had done wrong, and promised never again to transgress in like manner.

Thomas Jackson, (**33**), pp. 114–15.

Cobbett on the Methodists

There are, I know, persons who look upon the Methodists
... as friends of freedom. It is impossible they should be. They
are either fools or tricksters, or so nearly allied thereto, as to be
worthy of no consideration. Their heavenly gifts, their calls, their
inspirations, their feelings of grace at work within them, and
the rest of their canting gibberish, are a gross and outrageous
insult to common sense, and a great scandal to the country.
It is in vain that we boast of our enlightened state, while a
sect like this is increasing daily. It would seem that, at last,
men have fallen in love with ignorance of the most vulgar kind.
The very sound of the bellowings of one of these pretended sons
of inspiration is enough to create disgust in a hearer of sense.
The incoherent trash, the downright balderdash, that these
gifted brethren send forth surpasses all description, and it
really is a stain on the national character, that they should
find such multitudes to follow at their heels.

William Cobbett, *Weekly Political Register*, 1813, xxiii, col. 842.

The educational efforts of the Evangelicals

Has it been intended that these people, when taught to read,
should read nothing but Hannah MORE'S 'Sinful Sally,' and
Mrs. TRIMMER'S 'Dialogues'? Faith! The working classes of
the people have a relish for no such trash. They are not to be
amused by a recital of the manifold blessings of a state of things,
in which they have not half enough to eat, nor half enough to
cover their nakedness by day or to keep them from perishing
at night. They are not to be amused with the pretty stories about
'the bounty of Providence in making brambles for the purpose
of tearing of pieces of the sheep's wool, in order that the little
birds may come and get it to line their nests with to keep their
young ones warm!' Stories like these are not sufficient to fill the

minds of the working classes of the people. They want something more solid.'

ibid., 1817. xxxii, col. 417.

The religious philosophy of Wilberforce

Although Wilberforce today still has a high reputation as a social reformer and man of feeling it is the narrowness of his vision and the crude 'practicability' of his views that make the strongest impression. His vocation was that of a spiritual policeman.

[a] The tendency of religion in general to promote the temporal well being of political communities, is a fact which depends on such obvious and undeniable principles, and which is so forcibly inculcated by the history of the ages, that there can be no necessity of entering into a formal proof of its truth...

The peculiar excellence in this respect also of Christianity, *considered independently of its truth or falsehood*, has been recognised by many writers, who, to say the least, were not disposed to exaggerate its merits. Either or both of these propositions being admitted, the state of religion in a country at any given period ... immediately becomes a question of great *political* importance.

[b] Towards the close of the last century, the divines of the Established Church . . . professed to make it their chief object to inculcate the moral and practical precepts of Christianity which they conceived to have been too much neglected, but without sufficiently maintaining, or even without justly laying the grand foundation of a sinner's acceptance with God, or pointing out how the practical precepts of Christianity grow out of her peculiar doctrines and are inseparably connected with them. By this fatal error, the very genius and essential nature of Christianity imperceptibly underwent a change.

[c] But this world is not [the Christian's] resting place, here to the very last he must be a pilgrim and a stranger, a soldier whose warfare ends only with life, ever struggling and com-

batting the powers of darkness and with the temptations of the
world around him, and the still more dangerous hostilities of
internal depravity. The perpetual vicissitudes of this uncertain
state . . . teach him to look forward, almost with outstretched
neck, to that promised day, when he shall be completely delivered from the bondage of corruption, and sorrow and sighing
shall flee away.

[**d**] The kind of religion which we have recommended, *whatever opinion may be entertained concerning its truth* . . . must at least
be conceded to be the only one which is at all suited to make
impression upon the lower orders, by strongly interesting the
passions of the human mind. If it be thought that a system of
ethics may regulate the conduct of the higher classes, such a
one is altogether unsuitable to the lower, who must be worked
on by their affections, or they will not be worked on at all.

Let the Socinian and the moral teacher of Christianity come
forth and tell us what effect they have produced on the lower
orders. They themselves will hardly deny the inefficacy of their
instructions.

William Wilberforce, *A Practical View of the Religious System of
Professed Christians . . .*, 1797 (pp. 364–5, 382, 451, 409–10).

No room for the poor

*The fact that the working people of the cities—and especially of
London—neither had nor sought much contact with the Church was
regularly rediscovered throughout our period. The superficial contrast
with Goathland [**doc, 4**] is striking. Was the reality very different?
Young is best known as an agricultural publicist. He believed that
extensive commons and infrequent divine service were the roots of most
social evils. Here is his response to a request for a report on 'The present
state of public worship amongst the lowest classes of this Metropolis'.
His answer is brief.*

A very short space will give its contents, for in fact there is scarcely any such thing and the greatest evil I can complain of is, that as our churches are arranged at present, THERE CAN BE NO SUCH THING.

I have attended divine service in many of them with this particular view, and it afforded a subject of melancholy reflection to see nearly their whole space occupied by pews, to which the poor have no admittance; the aisles in many so narrow, as to contain very few as compared with the population of this great city, and none commodiously. In some churches, few or no benches to sit on and no mats to kneel on. A stranger would think that our churches were built, as indeed they are, only for the rich.

Arthur Young, *An Enquiry into the State of the Public Mind* . . ., 1798.

document 20

'To each his own ————'

*As we have noted in the case of Wilberforce [**doc. 18**], it is the narrowness of the eighteenth-century vision that so often surprises us, the bland assumption that the prevailing social order was the only possible one. Nor even for a clerical writer is religion the decisive factor: it provides added reasons for acceptance of things as they are. The order of the arguments is characteristic of the age.*

I (God knows) could not get my livelihood by labour, nor would the labourer find any solace or enjoyment in my studies. If we were to exchange conditions tomorrow, all the effect would be, that we should both be miserable and the work of both be worse done. Without debating therefore which of our two conditions was better to begin with . . . , one point is certain, that it is best for each to remain in his own.

If in comparing the different conditions of social life we bring religion into the account, the argument is still easier. Religion smooths all inequalities because it unfolds a prospect that makes all earthly distinction nothing.

W. Paley, Archdeacon of Carlisle, *Reasons for Contentment addressed to the Labouring Part of the British Public*, 1792.

A clerical catchpenny exposed

... Your title page, like that of the most prostituted hireling ... was a mere catchpenny, ... its object was not to lessen the hardships of the labourer but to secure to the rich and powerful their luxuries, extorted from the toil and miseries of the poor. ... I console myself in the reflection that the people have their season as well as the privileged few. Our winter has gone by and, full of hopes I now see spring approaching. With confidence we look forward to the protection of the God of All Nature, who by the deepest affliction often prepares us for the enjoyment of the greatest good, as a plentiful Autumn often succeeds the severest winter. O you who have already received the favours of heaven, look upon without despising those whom it has already oppressed with misfortune.

Revolutions prepare themselves in secret and it appears to me that some favourable change for us is likely to take place. Should it come to pass we shall not feel ourselves indebted either to the sophistry or the humanity of the Archdeacon of Carlisle. ...

Letter to ... Paley in Answer to his 'Reasons for Contentment' by A Poor Labourer, 1793.

'A quiet and somewhat lazy church ...'

'A quiet and somewhat lazy church, certainly not a persecuting one.' Not a flattering verdict by the eminent Whig politician but a just one for most of our period. One can understand why Churchmen were alarmed when the Whigs took power and discussed reform. The following extract is from a letter from Henry Brougham to Thomas Creevey, March 1823, the occasion being Hume's proposal to mount a House of Commons attack in the Established Church.

The people of this country are not prepared to give up the Church. For one—I am certainly not; and my reason is this. There is a vast mass of religion in the country, shaped in various forms and burning with various degrees of heat—from regular lukewarmness to Methodism. Some Church establishment this feeling must have; and I am quite clear that a much reformed Church of England is the safest form in which such an establishment can exist. It is a quiet and somewhat lazy Church: certainly not a persecuting one. Clip its wings of temporal power (which it unceasingly uses on behalf of a political slavery) and purify its more glaring abuses, and you are far better off than with a fanatical Church and Dominion of Saints, like that of the 17th century; or no Church at all and a Dominion of Sects, like that of America. . . . The Irish case is a great and an extreme one, and by keeping it strictly on its own grounds and abstaining from any topics common to both Churches, a bodyblow may be given. But if any means are afforded to the Church and its friends here of making common cause with the Irish fellows, I fear you convert a most powerful case into an ordinary one which must fall.

Quoted from *The Creevey Papers*, ed. John Gore, 1963, p. 220.

document 23
The inevitability of reform

There are some matters which will not wait for the investigation and deliberation of a commission, especially the question of a commutation of tithes, which must be settled at once, if it is to be settled at all in any other way than that of spoliation; but I do not see how the final determination of the questions concerning pluralities, and cathedral establishments, involving as they do so many complicated interests, can be made, with any prospect of a wise and equitable decision, except through the medium of a commission. At the same time some general principals may be agreed upon, and should be declared at once, as those upon which such commission is to proceed. This would satisfy all reasonable persons, and the unreasonable it is useless attempting to satisfy.

Parliament (i.e. the House of Commons) would probably be jealous of any distinct body legislating, even only initiatively, on Church matters; for they may be expected to be tenacious of their own privilege in this respect precisely in the degree in which they are unfit to exercise it. But we have a right to demand, either a convocation (which we do not wish for), or something which shall possess all the advantages of a convocation without the evils which were found to result from it under its old constitution. How to secure the good and to exclude the evil will be no easy problem. nevertheless we must attempt the solution of it; it is impossible that the Church (*in so far as it is of human institution*) can go on as it is.

Charles James Blomfield, Bishop of London to Archbishop Howley, 1832 (**53**, i, 206–7).

A crisis averted?

Would it be going too far to say, as in the proverb 'When the devil was sick . . .'? The fear of spoliation by the State was very great, the fear of revolutionary change was greater and churchmen tried to steer between Scylla and Charybdis. Peel's restrained proposals found favour with moderate and responsible churchmen [**doc, 23**]. *His irony, in the circumstances, is pardonable.*

When I came to office in 1834, the public mind had been very much excited by the demands for Church reform proceeding from very high authorities—carrying with them great weight, not only from official station in some instances (a Divinity Professor at Oxford, for example) but from their known attachment to the best interests of the Church. I wished enquiry to precede reformation—inquiry to be conducted exclusively by those who were believed by the public and by the Church to be sincere friends of the Establishment.

There appeared to be general satisfaction with this course of proceedings: the prospect of improvement, to be calmly and deliberately made, seemed to satisfy the friends of the Church, and to silence foolish and ignorant opponents. And then, *because* this result was produced—*because* the heat and excitement died away, in the confidence that the Church would undertake the task of reformation—it was discovered that there was no need to reform at all, and that any practical proceeding, of any nature whatever, towards it ought to be vehemently opposed. I have some communications on the necessity and advantage of Church reform (when it was at a distance), which surprise me, now that I refer to them, at the excessive scruples of the authors. . . .

Sir Robert Peel to the Bishop of London 1838 (**52**, i, 210).

document 25
The unseen world encroaches . . .

The genius of the Georgian Church was a pragmatic one. It judged itself—when it considered judgment needed—by such criteria as nominal membership, formal participation and acquiescence in the political and social system of the day as 'the best of all possible worlds'. Newman's vital, spiritual view of the Church could hardly be 'lived out' in such a context. His ultimate secession was inevitable.

Such is the City of God, The Holy Church Catholic throughout the world, manifested in and acting through what is called in each country the Church visible; which visible Church really depends solely on it, on the invisible,—not on civil power, not on princes or any child of man, not on endowments, not on its numbers, not on anything that is seen, unless indeed heaven can depend on earth, eternity on time, Angels on men, the dead on the living. The unseen world through God's secret power and mercy encroaches upon this; and the Church that is seen is just that portion of it by which it encroaches; and thus though the visible Churches of the Saints in this world seem rare, and scattered to and fro, like islands in the sea, they are in truth but the tops of the everlasting hills, high and vast and deeply rooted, which a deluge covered.

From an Anglican sermon of J. H. Newman, quoted (**9**)

'The Irvingite gift'

The extract below is part of an answer given by Dr Thomas Arnold, the famous Headmaster of Rugby and leading Liberal Churchman, to an enquirer about his attitude to Irving and the phenomenon of 'speaking with tongues'. The document reflects the apprehension caused even in the most balanced minds by the crisis in Church and State, the recent revolutions in Europe and the cholera epidemic then raging. The year was 1832.

If the thing be real, I should take it merely as a sign of the coming of the day of the Lord—the only use, as far as I can make out, that ever was derived from the gift of tongues. I do not see that it was ever made a vehicle of instruction, or ever superseded the study of tongues, but that it was merely a sign of the power of God; a man being for the time transformed into a mere instrument to utter sounds which he himself understood not. . . . However, whether this be a real sign or no, I believe that 'the day of the Lord' is coming—that is, the termination of one of the great [ages] of the human race, whether the final one of all or not: that I believe, no created being ever knows or can know. The termination of the Jewish Age in the first century, and of the Roman in the fifth and sixth, were each marked by the same concurrence of calamities, wars, tumults, pestilences, earthquakes, etc, all marking the time of one of God's peculiar seasons of visitation. . . . My sense of the evil of the times, and to what prospects I am bringing up my children, is overwhelmingly bitter. All the moral and physical world appears so exactly to announce the coming of 'the great day of the Lord'—that is a period of fearful visitation, to terminate the existing state of things—whether to terminate the whole existence of the human race, neither man nor angel knows—that no entireness of private happiness can possibly close my mind against the sense of it.

Quoted in Martineau (**79**), ii, 458–9.

A midcentury retrospect

The raising of acceptable standards was more than a little due to the Oxford Movement. Note also the interesting assessment of Methodism.

In character, habits, attainments, social position and general reputation, the ordinary clergyman of 1860 is very different from the clergyman of 1810. . . .

The most obvious difference is the low standard of character and duties which then prevailed among clergymen compared to what is now generally expected of them. Fifty years ago, a decent and regular performance of Divine Service on Sundays was almost all that anyone looked for in a clergyman; if this were found, most people were satisfied. The clergyman might be non-resident, a sportsman, a farmer, neglectful of all study, a violent politician, a bon vivant, or a courtier; but if he performed in person, or by deputy, that which now usurped the name of his 'duty', that was enough. We find Bishops of this period, in their Charges, insisting upon duties and qualifications which are now taken for granted, and deprecating practices which are now almost unheard of.

What were the causes which produced this low standard of clerical character? They appear to have been mainly these:— First, the general laxity of the eighteenth century, not much improved by the *external irritation of Methodism*, and extending into the nineteenth. Secondly, the strong Conservative feeling engendered in England by the French Revolution, which clung to things as they were because they were so; upheld the rights, while it repudiated the duties of property, and stigmatized reform as sedition and earnestness as enthusiasm. Dr Copleston wrote in 1814, 'The leading partisans who assumed that title [High Churchmen] appear to me to be only occupied with the thought of converting the property of the Church, to their private advantage, leaving the duties of it to be performed how they can.' Thirdly, that legacy of the Reformation which had never been substantially altered—a system of benefices most inadequately endowed in the great majority of cases, but richly in a few, entailing all the evils of non-residence, pluralities, and proprietary chapels, and by the unequal distribution of revenues, inflicting upon the Church at once the discomfort of bc ng extremely poor, and the discredit of being extremely rich.

A. Blomfield (53), pp. 57–8.

Portrait of a midcentury archdeacon

'*The Warden*' *written in 1855 and '*Barchester Towers*' (1857) are studies of clerical life and character so perceptive and plausible as to have been widely taken as portraits of actual persons. They are artistic masterpieces that must be awarded honorary documentary status. Here Trollope is writing of the qualities of an archdeacon.*

He is diligent, authoritative, and, as his friends particularly boast, judicious. His great fault is an overbearing assurance of the virtues and claims of his order, and his great foible is an equally strong confidence in the dignity of his own manner and the eloquence of his own words. He is a moral man, believing the precepts which he teaches, and believing also that he acts up to them; though we cannot say that he would give up his coat to the man who took his cloak, or that he is prepared to forgive his brother even seven times. He is severe enough in exacting his dues, considering that any laxity in this respect would endanger the security of the church; and, could he have his way, he would consign to darkness and perdition, not only every individual reformer, but every committee and every commission that would even dare to ask a question respecting the appropriation of church revenues.

Anthony Trollope, *The Warden*, chap. 2.

Hunt out the poor . . .

In these extracts Bishop Blomfield comes face to face with the fact of 'Two Nations'. The desire to teach the poor is sincere enough though the means envisaged are perhaps feeble. What the Bishop does not grasp is the depth of the gulf, the degree of alienation.

[a] I feel very strongly the desirableness of increasing the ministrations of the clergy amongst the poor, who will not attend our fine churches, even where there is room for them. Most of the incumbents of the great London parishes have extra services for the poor in their school-rooms, which are well attended; but more is needed in the way of personal intercourse and instruction. The Scripture readers have worked very well in a subordinate capacity; but we want some persons, deacons, or lay-teachers, who will hunt out the poor at their own homes on Sundays, the only day on which they are to be met with there. I have more than once pressed this on some of the clergy. . . .

[b] I entertain some doubts as to churches to be used exclusively by the poor, a provision which seems to mark more strongly the already too wide distinction between them and the upper classes; and it certainly has not answered my expectations in Bethnal Green, where there are no pew-rents nor appropriated sittings in the new churches. The truth is that what we want is home visitation and house lectures to bring to the poor a knowledge of the first truths and principles of religion, and so to prepare them to value the advantages of public worship when offered to them.

A. Blomfield (**53**).

Religion and the costermonger

Henry Mayhew (1812–1887) dramatist, journalist and social investigator published a collection of articles in 1851 under the title 'London

Labour and London Poor'. They were many times reissued, supple-
mented, anthologised and have even, in recent years, been used as radio
scripts. Mayhew's great gift was the ability to capture the living
speech of his subjects.

'The costers have no religion at all, and very little notion or
none at all, of what religion or a future state is. . . . But I'm
satisfied that if the costers were to profess themselves of some
religion tomorrow they would all become Roman Catholics,
every one of them. This is the reason;—London costers live
very often in the same courts and streets as the poor Irish, and
if the Irish are sick, be sure there comes to them the priest, the
Sisters of Charity—they *are* good women—and some other
ladies. Many a man that's not a Catholic, has rotted and died
without any good person near him. Why, I've lived a good while
in Lambeth, and there wasn't one coster in a hundred, I'm
satisfied, knew so much as the rector's name,—though Mr
Dalton's a very good man. But the reason I was telling you of,
sir, is that the costers reckon *that* religion's the best that gives
the most in charity, and they think the Catholics do this.'

'St Pauls . . . ? A church, sir; so I've heard. I never was in a
church. O, yes, I've heard of God; he made heaven and earth;
I never heard of his making the sea; that's another thing, and
you can best learn about that at Billingsgate . . . Jesus Christ?
Yes. I've heard of him. Our Redeemer? Well, I only wish I
could redeem my Sunday togs from my uncle's.'

'I never heard about Christianity; but if a cove was to fetch
me a lick of the head, I'd give it him again whether he was a
big 'un or a little 'un. . . . Do I understand what behaving to
your neighbour is?—In coorse I do. If a feller as lives next me
wanted a basket of mine as I wasn't using, why, he might have
it. . . . No; I never heard about this here creation you speaks
about. In coorse God Almighty made the world, and the poor
bricklayers' labourers built the houses arterwards. . . . I have
heered a little about our Saviour,—they seem to say he were a
goodish kind of man; but if he says as how a cove is to forgive
a fellow as hits you, I should say he knowed nothing about it.'

Mayhew's London (**8o**) 54, 57, 8o.

Bibliography

GENERAL IDEAS

1 Stark, W. *The Sociology of Religion*, Routledge and Kegan Paul, (3 vols), 1966–68. An invaluable study of 'the social forms which Christianity has assumed through the ages' together with the widest possible range of comparative material.

THE EUROPEAN BACKGROUND

2 Cragg, G. R. *The Church and the Age of Reason*, Penguin (Pelican) 1960.

3 Vidler, A. R. *The Church in an Age of Revolution*, Penguin (Pelican) 1961. Each of these has its own useful booklist.

THE BRITISH BACKGROUND

4 Halévy, E. *A History of the English People in 1815*, Book iii, *Religion and Culture*, 1924; Benn paperback 1961. An unprejudiced French view of the complexities of British religious life. Comprehensive bibliography.

5 Williams, B. *The Whig Supremacy*, 2nd edn, Oxford University Press, 1962.

6 Watson, J. S. *The Reign of George III*, Oxford University Press, 1960.

7 Woodward, E. L. *The Age of Reform*, (corrected edn,) Oxford University Press, 1946. These three consecutive volumes of the Oxford History of England have excellent bibliographies of older material.

ANGLICANISM

8 Byng, J. *The Torrington Diaries*, ed. C. B. Andrews, Eyre & Spottiswoode, 1954. A most interesting record of (among other things) the religious apprehensions of 'a plain blunt man' of the upper classes.

9 Faber, G. *Oxford Apostles*, Penguin, 1954. Chap. 3 is a masterly survey of 'The Parties in the Church'.

111

10 Sykes, N. *Church and State in the XVIIIth Century*, 1934. It is the work of Professor Sykes more than anything else that has led to the more favourable views of the Georgian Church that now prevail.

11 Turberville, A. S. ed., *Johnson's England*, Oxford University Press, 1952, (2 vols.) Vol i, ch. 2, 'The Church' by Norman Sykes has a bibliography with much unusual matter for the advanced student.

12 Welsby, P. A. ed., *Sermons and Society*, Penguin, 1970. An anthology of Anglican sermons on social topics from the days of Latimer (d. 1555) to those of Hensley Henson (d. 1947).

13 Woodforde, J. *The Diary of a Country Parson*, Oxford University Press, 1949—(Selections ed. by John Beresford.) The self-revelation of a representative and utterly undistinguished but thoroughly charming clergyman. Covers the period to 1803.

DISSENT

14 Davies, H. *The English Free Churches*, Oxford University Press, (Home University Library), 1963.

15 Watson, Steven, 'Dissent and toleration', in *The Silver Renaissance: Essays in eighteenth-century English History*, ed. A. Natan, Macmillan, 1961.

16 Payne, E. A. *The Free Church Tradition in the Life of England*, Hodder & Stoughton, 1965.

17 Thompson, E. P. *The Making of the English Working Class* Gollancz 1963 rev. edn, Penguin (Pelican), 1968. See especially Part I sections 2 and 3 'Christian and Apollyon' and 'Satan's Strongholds'. This splendidly impassioned work is a veritable encyclopaedia of working-class life 1780–1832. It is full of thought-provoking suggestions and controversial appraisals, especially about Methodism.

18 Williams, E. N. *A Documentary History of England*, Penguin (Pelican), 1965, vol. ii. Text and exposition of the Toleration Act which was both the charter and the prison of English Dissent.

SUPERSTITIONS AND PREJUDICES

19 Henderson, W. *Notes on the Folklore of the Northern Counties of England*, 2nd edn, 1879. Despite its title this book contains material from all parts of the country and is the standard source—usually without acknowledgement—for much popular writing on folklore.

20 Smith, A. W. 'Popular religion', *Past and Present*, 40, July 1968.

21 Vaux, J. E. *Church Folklore*, 1894. This gives a real insight into popular religion but also contains much of mere curiosity value. It could be the basis of a useful work.

ROMAN CATHOLICS

22 Norman E. R. *Anti-Catholicism in Victorian England*, Allen & Unwin, 1968.

23 Smith S. *Peter Plymley's Letters*, 1807. A witty and pugnacious defence of Roman Catholic claims to enjoy equal civil rights which also contains valuable observations on Anglican life and personalities in general. Sample 'Letters' often appear in collections of essays.

24 Watkins, E. I. *Roman Catholicism in England*, Oxford University Press (Home University Library), 1957.

THE JEWS

25 Gidney, W. T. *The History of the London Society for Promoting Christianity among the Jews*, 1908. This work contains many interesting sidelights on religious life in the early part of the nineteenth century especially of Evangelical—High Church—Dissenter relations.

26 Henriques, U. R. Q. 'The Jewish Emancipation controversy in nineteenth century Britain', *Past and Present*, 40, July 1968.

27 *Reports of the Committee of the London Society* (1–20), 2nd edn, 1819.

METHODISM

28 Andrews, S. *Methodism* Longman (Seminar Studies), 1970.

29 Davies, R. E. *Methodism*, Penguin (Pelican), 1963. Reverses the approach of Wearmouth (**36**) and seeks to consider Methodism as an example of a recurrent phenomenon in Church history, the orthodox pressure group. Has been known to bewilder elderly Methodists who thought Wesley was their founder.

30 *Memorials of Early Methodism in the Easingwold Circuit, by a Layman*, 1872.

31 Hammond, J. L. and Hammond, M. B. *The Town Labourer*, 1925. Chapter 13 examines Methodism's political involvements.

Davies was very misleading here!

113

32 Hobsbawm, E. J. 'Methodism and the threat of the French Revolution', *History Today*, Feb. 1957. Effectively questions the simplistic though timehallowed view that Wesley saved England from Jacobin revolution.

33 Jackson, T. *Life of the Rev. Robert Newton*, 1855.

34 Nettel, R. 'Folk elements in nineteenth century Puritanism', in *Folklore*, 80, Winter 1969. A study in the relationship of religion and popular culture.

35 Plumb, J. H. *England in the Eighteenth Century*, Penguin (Pelican), 1950. The brief chapter on Methodism is an exercise in verbal assault. A useful corrective to any traditional treatment of the subject. E. P. Thompson (**17**) takes the case for the prosecution even further and seeks to expose a sinister face behind Methodism's traditionally benign mask.

36 Wearmouth, J. R. *Methodism and the Common People*, Epworth Press 1945. Discusses Methodism in its eighteenth century social context reaffirming the movement's approval of its own achievements. An oft-quoted source of social facts.

37 Wesley, J. *Selected Letters*, ed. F. C. Gill, Epworth Press, 1956.

SECTARIAN MOVEMENTS

The literature in this field is very uneven in scope and quality. The best books are the large general treatments, e.g. (1) For the link between sectarianism and social conflict in the modern world see:

38 Lanternari, V. *The Religions of the Oppressed*, trans. from Italian, Knopf, 1963; Mentor 1965.

For the background in our period see:

39 Hobsbawm, E. J. *The Age of Revolution* (Weidenfeld, 1962), Mentor, 1962 Ch. 12 surveys the religious aspects of social ideologies.

40 Matthews, R. *English Messiahs*, Methuen, 1936. Biographical studies of a selection of imposters/victims of religious delusion. Simple psychological approach.

41 Montgomery, J. *Abodes of Love*, Putnam, 1962. A compilation rather than an organised treatment, but useful nonetheless.

42 Rogers, P. G. *The Battle in Bossenden Wood*, Oxford University Press, 1961. A modern treatment of the fascinating 'Sir William Courteney'.

43 Roth, C. *The Nephew of the Almighty*, Goldston, 1933. A leading Jewish historian on Richard Brothers. Thompson (**17** *passim*) relates Brothers and Southcott to the political and social scene.

EVANGELICALS AND JACOBINS

(4) (9) (17) are especially useful here as is (**31**), ch. 11.

44 Bray, J. F. *A Voyage from Utopia*, Lawrence & Wishart, 1957. Social and political satire by one of precursors of Marx gives a brutal pen picture of Christianity as seen by a working man.

45 Budd, S. 'Loss of faith 1850–1950', *Past and Present*, 36, April 1967. Discusses the secularist critique of Christianity.

46 Hammond, J. L. and Hammond, B. *The Village Labourer*, 1927 edn. Chapter 8, a general consideration of the role of religion in social life, discusses Wilberforce as oppressor of the poor.

47 Harrison, B. 'Religion and recreation in nineteenth century England', *Past and Present*, 36, Dec. 1967, discusses the lack of working class appreciation for the activities of 'do-gooders'.

48 Jaeger, M., *Before Victoria*: *Changing standards of behaviour 1787–1837*, Penguin, 1970.

49 Kiernan, V. G. 'Evangelicalism and the French Revolution', *Past and Present*, 1 Feb. 1952.

50 Summerson, J. *Georgian London* (Plerades, 1945), Penguin (Pelican), 1962. Chapter 16 'Church and State' puts the 1818 church building programme into its social and architectural background.

51 White, R. J. *Life in Regency England*, Batsford, 1963. Chapter 8 'The Puritan Revival' is useful, despite its question-begging title.

THE HIGH CHURCH REVIVAL

(3) (7) and (9) should also be consulted on this topic.

52 Best, G. F. A. 'The Whigs and the Church Establishment in the age of Grey', *History*, June 1960.

53 Blomfield, A. *A Memoir of C. J. Blomfield*, 1863, 2 vols. A study of the bishop who steered the Church through the reform crisis of the 1830s. The source of most standard textbook anecdotes of episcopal laxity etc.

54 Bosworth, R. N. *The Restoration of the Apostles and Prophets*, 1888. An account of the Catholic Apostolic Church for which see also (**1**) above.

55 Inglis, K. J. 'Patterns of religious worship 1851', *Journal of Ecclesiastical History*, 11, 1960.

56 Newman, J. H. *Apologia pro vita sua* (1864) Dent, Everyman edn, 1955. Every student of this period should wrestle with the supple, not to say slippery mind of Newman who as a child speculated as to whether he might not be an angel in disguise. It remains an interesting hypothesis.

57 Smith, Sydney, *Three Letters to Archdeacon Singleton*, 1837. Racy comment on the reform proposals by celebrated clerical wit.

58 Stunt, T. F. C. 'Two nineteenth-century movements', *Evangelical Quarterly* 37, no. 4, 1965. Discusses the common concerns of Brethren and Tractarians.

59 Webster, A. B. *Joshua Watson*, S.P.C.K., 1954. Study of a 'pre-Oxford' High Churchman.

SUPPLEMENTARY REFERENCES

60 Addison, Joseph. *Spectator* No. 112, 9 July 1711.

61 Anon. *Anecdotes and Manners of a Few Ancient and Modern Oddities*, York, 1806.

62 Ashton, T. S. *Economic History of England in the Eighteenth Century*, new edn, Methuen, 1955.

63 Aubrey, John, *Remains of Gentilisme and Judaisme*, annotated by J. Britten, Folklore Society, 1881.

64 Bamford, Samuel, *Passages in the Life of a Radical, and Early Days*, ed. H. Dunckley (Verax), Fisher Unwin, 1905, 2 vols.

65 Bett, H. *English Myths and Traditions*, Batsford 1952.

66 Brantome, Abbé de. *Vie des dames galantes*, trans. by A. Brown as *The Lives of Gallant Ladies*, Panther, 1965.

67 Brontë, Charlotte. *Shirley*, 1849.

68 Green, Martin, ed. *Casanova in London*, Mayflower, 1969.

69 Courtenay, M. A. *Cornish Feasts and Folklore*, Penzance, 1894.

70 Coleman, Terry. *The Railway Navvies* (Hutchinson, 1965), Penguin, 1968.

71 Coleridge, S. T. *Table Talk*, ed. H. N. Coleridge, 1835, 2 vols.

72 Cowper, William. *Letters*, Oxford University Press, World's Classics.

73 Firth, C. H. *Oliver Cromwell and the Rule of the Puritans in England* (1900), Oxford University Press, World's Classics.

74 Hammond, J. L. and Hammond, B. *Lord Shaftesbury*, 1923.

75 Hibbert, Christopher, *King Mob: Lord George Gordon*, Longmans, 1958.
76 Home, G. *Evolution of an English Town*, 1915.
77 Hunt, R. *Popular Romances of the West of England*, 1881.
78 Maclean, Fitzroy. *A Person from England*, Cape, 1958.
79 Martineau, Harriet. *History of the Thirty Years Peace* (28 vols, 1849–50), Bell, Bohn edn, 4 vols, 1877.
80 Mayhew, Henry. *Mayhew's London*, ed. P. Quennell, Kimber, 1951.
81 Ritson, J. *The Romance of Primitive Methodism*, 1911.
82 Selley, E. *Village Trade Unions in Two Centuries*, 1919.
83 Smollett, Tobias. *Humphry Clinker*, 1771.
84 Tongue, Ruth L. *Somerset Folklore*, Folklore Society, 1965.
85 Truman, C. S. *The Hamlet of Mile End Town*, Stepney Borough Council (Public Library Dept), 1963.
86 Ware, T. *The Orthodox Church*, Penguin (Pelican), 1963.
87 Young, Arthur. *A General View of the Agriculture of Lincolnshire*, Board of Agriculture, 1799.
88 Wesley, J. *Letters* ed. Telford 8 vols, 1931,

Index

Abgarus, Letter to, 39
Acts of Parliament
  for Fifty New Churches, 53
  Schism, 3, 16
  Toleration, 5, 16
Agapemone, 49
Anne, Queen, 3, 9, 53
anticlericalism, 22
Arianism, 4
Arnold, Dr T., 32, 106
Atkinson, Matthew, 29
Austen, Jane, 9
Aylesbury (Bucks), 90

Bamford, Samuel, 39, 92
Banyard, John, 49
Baptists, doc. 5, doc. 6
'Barchester Towers', 108
Bateman, Thos, 35
Berkeley (Bp), 4
Bethnal Green, 109
Billingsgate, 110
Blomfield (Bp), 104
Bossenden Wood (Kent), 47
Brantome, Abbe de, 94
Bray, J. F., 55
Brethren (Plymouth), 6, 64, 73
Bridges, Wm., 49
Briggs, Dr K. M., 93
British Israel, 47
Brontë, C., 31, 84
Brothers, Richard, 6, 29, 45–7, 57, 73
Brougham, 61, 103
Buchan, Elspeth, 44
Bulteel, H., 66
Bunting, J., 97
Bunyan, J., 16
Butler (Bp), 4, 17, 33
Byng, J., 11

Cardale, J. B., 67
Carlile, R., 55
Casanova, 41
Catholic Apostolic Church, 67
Census (of Religious Worship 1851), 7, 71
Challoner (Bp), 30
Chalmers, Thos, 66
Chartism, 67
Chipping Norton, 23
Christian Science, 75
'Clapham Sect', 67
Clarke, S., 4
Cobbett, Wm, 51, 53, 55, 72, doc. 16, doc. 17
'Cokelers', 49
Coleridge, S. T., 54, 59
Convocation, 3, 6, 27
Cowper, Wm., 30, 81
Crawfoot, Jas., 40
Cromwell, O., 15, 16, 53
Cumberland, R., 31

Darby, J. N., 64
'Dean and Chapter', 19
Defoe, Daniel, 86
Deism, 4, 29, 55
Delamere (Ches.), 40
Dissenters, 4, 6, 15–18, 21, 23, 28, doc. 7, doc. 8
Drummond, H., 66

Easingwold (Yorks), 37, 96
Ecclesiastical Commissioners, 60
Ecclesiastical Titles Bill (1851), 7
Eliot, G., 15, 18
'enthusiasm', 4
Erastianism, 3, 12
Evangelicals, 5, 12, 42, 51, 63

Index

Exhibition (1851), 71

Feathers Tavern Petition (1772), 11
Fielding, H., 10, 15
folklore, 72
Fox, C. J., 16, 59
Franciscans, 5, 24
Froude, J. H., 63

George I, 9, 82
George III, 17, 46
Gibbon, E., 9
Girling, Mary Ann, 49
Glasgow, 66
Goathland (Yorks), 83
Goldsmith, O., 72, 82
Gordon, Lord G., 29, 47
Gordon Riots, 24
Grey, Earl, 6

Hawksmoor, N., 3
Hoadley (Bp), 4, 74
Hogarth, 24
Holles, Daniel, 29
Howley (Abp), 104
Hume, David, 4

Ireland, Church of, 61, 64
Irvingites, 6, 49, 64–7, 73

Jackson, T., 34
Jacobinism, 5, 51
Jehovah's Witnesses, 41
Jews, 8, 24, 30–2
Johnson, S., 29, 53
'Jumpers', 49

Keble, J., 6, 61
Ken (Bp), 8, 13, 74
Kingsley, Chas, 55

Lambeth, 110
Lastingham (Yorks), 10
Latitudinarianism, 11, 56, 72
Latter Day Saints, 66
Law, Wm, 4, 11, 71, 82
Lee, 'Mother' Ann, 44
Leslie, Shane, 62, 64
Levi, David, 31

Liverpool, 97
Loveless, G., 15, 17, 23
Lovett, Wm, 55
Ludd, 97

Madan, Martin, 73
Magee (Abp), 65
Manessah, J., 30
Manchester, 60
Manning (Cardinal), 62
Marsh (Bp), 58
Mayhew, H., 24, 110
Methodists, 5, 28, 33–40, 72, 73, 103, 107
Middleton (Lancs), 92
More, Hannah, 53, 99
Muggletonians, 6, 43

'nativism', 39, 48
navvies, 28
Newman, J. H., 18, 28, 62, 64, 106
Newton, R., 34, doc. 15
nonjurors, 4, 13, 14, 27, 64, 82
Norfolk (11th Duke of), 29

Occasional Conformity, 3, 16, 21, 72, 87
Oxford Movement, 62, 64

Paine, T., 54, 63, 85
Paley (Archd.), 102
'Papal aggression', 7
'Peculiars', 49
Peel, Sir Robert, 60, 105
Percival, Spencer, Jnr., 63
Peterborough Questions, 58
Pickering (Yorks), 39
Plymouth (see Brethren)
polygamy, 73
'Primitives', 21, 35, 39, 73
Prince, H. J., 49
Protestantism, 41
Pugin, 53 fn.
Pusey, 57

Quakers, 8, 23, 24

Raskelf (Yorks), 37
Revolution, French, 5, 42
'Rights of Man', 63

272

Ripon (Yorks.), 60
Roman Catholics, 4 6, 14, 59, 110
Robespierre, 56

Sancroft (Abp), 13
Scotland, Church of, 66
Secker (Bp), 95
Shaftesbury, Lord, 63
Sharp, Granville, 57
Shylock, 31
Simeon, Chas, 52
Smith, Joseph, 48
Smith, Sydney, 22, 53, 88
Smollett, T., 8, 30
Societies
　—for Promotion of Christian Know-
　　　ledge, 3
　—for Propagation of the Gospel, 3
　—for Reformation of Manners, 3
Socinianism, 4
Southcott, J., 6, 43–5, 57, 73
Spiritualism, 55, 75
Staffordshire figures, 22, 92
Stanhop, Hester, 48

Thornton, H., 57
tithes, 22, 61, 88–9
Tolpuddle (Dorset), 88
Tom, J. N., 47–9
Tomline (Bp), 95
Tories, 3, 6

Tractarianism, 6, 20, 63
Trollope, A., 108

Unitarianism, 4, 55, 63
Urquhart, Thos., 17

Van Mildert (Bp), 58
Vasey, Rev. T., 38
Victoria Institute, 64
Venn, 57

Walworth, 49
Warburton (Bp), 18, 64, doc. 1
Ward, J., 45
'Warden, The', 108
'Waterloo churches', 53 fn.
Wesley, J., 5, 33, 50, 73, doc. 13
Whigs, 4, 103
Whiston, 4
Whitby (Yorks.), 37
Whitty, Rev. Irvine, 61
Wicklow (Ireland), 64
Wilberforce, Wm, 10, 51–6, doc. 18
William III, 9
Wolfe, Joseph, 32
Wollstonecraft, Mary, 44
Woodhouse, F., 67
Wroe, John, 45

Yonge, Charlotte, 93
Young, A., 11, doc. 19